# Extreme Weather

# Extreme Weather

by Peter Bunyard

Floris Books

First published in 2006 by Floris Books
© 2006 Peter Bunyard

British Library CIP Data available

ISBN-10  0-86315-568-5
ISBN-13  978-086315-568-0

Produced in Poland by Polskabook

# Contents

To Jimena, *mi vida,* and to my children and grandchildren

# Acknowledgments

Many thanks to Floris Books for their enormous help in the preparation of the book and especially to Christopher Moore, who gave up much of his time in helping me with ideas and structure. And thanks, too, to Ulrike Fischer for her indefatigable help in providing the illustrations and working on the way the book should look, as well as to all those at Floris who made the book possible and kept me to deadlines.

Throughout the years I have been fortunate to have the support of Teddy Goldsmith and I thank him from the bottom of my heart for helping me in my attempts to bring climate issues to the fore, both in *The Ecologist* and in my travels, especially to Colombia where forest and mountains meet, and where its geographic position between Pacific and Caribbean gives it a special, incomparable place in the world of nature.

I have many friends in Colombia who have helped me in my travels and have made possible the many lectures on climate and rainforest issues that I have given in recent years. Carolina Vásquez, as well as her companions in the Fundación Construir Futuro y Bienestar, have been pillars of strength and have always had faith in my ability to express myself in my faltering Spanish. I also thank Tom Rivett-Carnac and his father for their help in Colombia, enabling me through their foundation, Enable Change.

I am grateful too, to the many climatologists who have had the patience to inform me, including Richard Betts of the Hadley Centre, Peter Cox of the Institute for Ecology and Hydrology, and Germán Poveda of the National University in Medellín, Colombia.

Finally, I would like to express my thanks to my children for putting up with me, to Simon and Ruth Bunyard in Massachusetts for always helping me out, and to Jimena, in Colombia, who has stuck to me through thick and thin.

# Introduction

Climate change is hitting harder and much faster than antici-pated, and we are increasingly experiencing extreme weather conditions around the globe. We thought we had time, at least the next fifty years to pull back from the brink of irreversible change, but now it seems we may well be hurtling towards global catastrophe. The problem is that all the extraordinary climatic events that have been occurring over the past few years — the melting of the Arctic ice, the violent hurricanes that have struck the Caribbean, the unparalleled drought in Amazonia in 2005, repeated in 2006, the melting of glaciers, tropical storms where they have never before been recorded, even the July 2006 heat-waves in Europe and in California, with an increasing number of heat-stroke related deaths — can all be considered part of natural variability, therefore little to do with human activities. That gives some of us, including the US Administration, an excuse to sit on our hands and wait for definitive answers, the fabled 'fiddling while Rome burns.'

In severe weather terms, the year 2005 was exceptional. That year, the number of Atlantic hurricanes, some twenty-seven in the designated 'hurricane season' between June and the end of November, well exceeded the total of twenty-one in the previous record year of 1933. It was also well above the expected average count, since 1995, of around thirteen named storms per year (com-pared to 8.6 during the preceding twenty-five years). Hard on the

*LEFT:*
*Can we afford to keep looking away and to pretend that what we put into our atmosphere is not also what we breathe and eat, in the widest sense? Scientists all over the world now agree that $CO_2$ pollution has come to haunt us in multiple and escalating ways: through droughts, floods, hur-ricanes, storms and consequences we might not have guessed at yet. A suburban area near Chelyabinsk, Russia. [Yaroslav Mishin]*

*NEXT PAGE:*
*Saharan dust, and pollution over Atlantic and North Sea countries [NASA]*

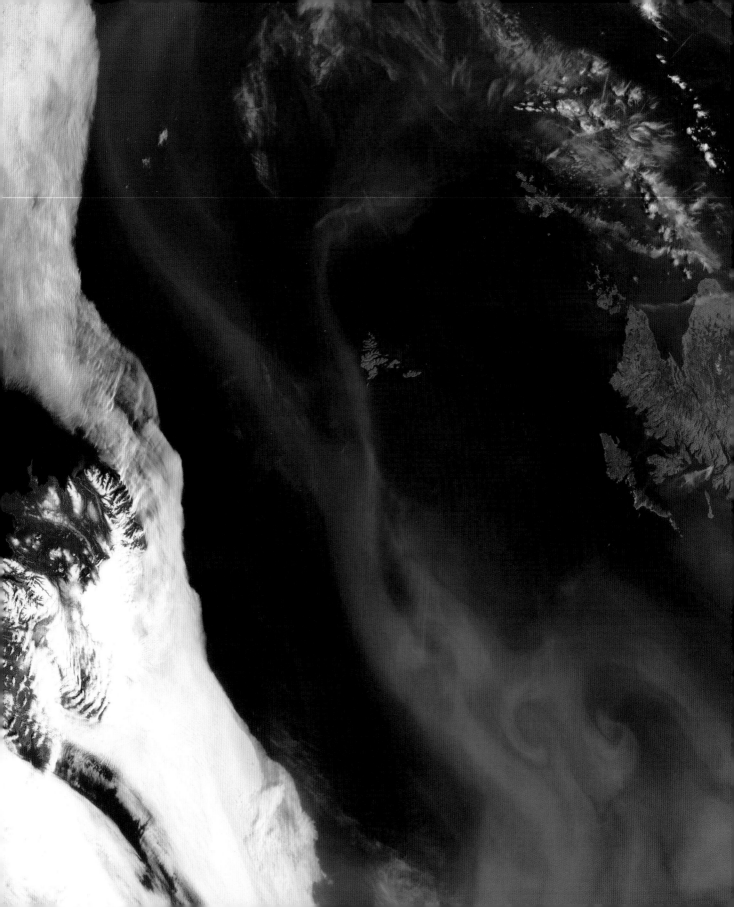

heels of Katrina came Rita and Wilma, both, like their predecessor, causing billions of dollars worth of damage. Furthermore, the very first day of December, a record in itself given its lateness in the year, a hurricane was spawned in the Caribbean. That could only mean that the surface temperatures of the ocean were still high enough to give a cyclonic storm the energy it needed to develop into a hurricane. 2005 was also the year when we discovered that the Gulf Stream had faltered by 30 percent, a massive change in terms of the energy transported in the form of warm surface waters to the North Atlantic. It was the year in which the Amazon Basin suffered an unprecedented drought that left millions of fish dead and whole communities without the means to transport themselves for food and medicines.

To make matters worse, more Arctic ice than ever before melted in the summer of 2005, exposing ever more open sea, and because the sea absorbs the sun's energy rather than reflects it, the sea warms up still more and so prevents as much ice forming compared with the previous year. In 2005, we also discovered that global warming had caused melting of the upper permafrost layers in Siberia, allowing vast quantities of methane to be emitted. Since methane, weight per weight, has a greenhouse effect sixty times that of carbon dioxide over a period of one hundred years, such releases do not bode well for our efforts to curb greenhouse gas emissions.

Such dramatic changes and weather events look likely to be a pattern for the future. If so, that will have dire consequences for the planet's climate. Indeed, the present situation is looking ever more serious, the sum of all such dramatic climate events indicating that we may be reaching 'tipping points' from where there is no easy going back, even were we to pull out all the stops and halt our greenhouse gas emissions overnight. That we are already at the cliff's edge is a serious possibility, and we won't know till we literally tip over.

The extreme weather resulting from climate change can threaten all our best endeavours. It can cause ferocious floods or swamp coastal areas; it can trigger heatwaves and droughts; it can give rise to storms powerful enough to destroy cities as Hurricane Katrina did to New Orleans in 2005. Climate change can make life miserable for millions of people; it is the harbinger of destroyed crops, famines, epidemics, floods, of lands lost to the rising seas.

Today, we are experiencing the consequences of an average global temperature rise of 0.6°C. If global temperatures were to rise over the land mass by as much as 10°C within a century, as predicted in some of the climate models of the UK Met Office's Hadley Centre for Climate Prediction, we can expect crop-killing heatwaves, with the spectre of mass starvation, torrents of rain and ferocious floods, violent storms, droughts on an unimaginable scale, disease epidemics as vectors, such as mosquitoes, move into higher latitudes, with even malaria or dengue fever perhaps re-visiting the United Kingdom. Nowhere will be exempt from the deleterious impact of climate change, not even those countries, or rather governments, in denial, such as the United States. Already, looking from the hard end, where insurance costs actually represent the price paid for disasters, the Insurance Information Institute records that of the eleven most expensive natural disasters in recent world history, eight have occurred in the past four years along the US Gulf coast in the form of extreme weather events. The ruinous hurricane season of 2005 is estimated to have cost nearly 60 billion US dollars in insurance terms, figures that were scarcely imaginable in the past.

The major insurance group, Lloyds of London, is certainly starting to take climate change seriously. After issuing a report in June 2006 called *Climate Change, Adapt or Bust,* the group sponsored a gathering on climate change in order to get the message across. According to a BBC Business report by Clare Davidson, Lloyds' directors were plainspoken in their warnings. 'If we don't take action now to understand the changing nature of our planet and its impact, we will face extinction,' said Rolf Tolle, Lloyd's franchise performance director. And Bill McGuire, a geohazard specialist at University College London, warned members, 'You haven't seen nothing yet, climate change will come to dominate everything we do.'

A recent report from the New Economics Foundation (August 2006) quotes the alarming estimate that in the 1990s some two billion people globally were affected by extreme weather and other natural disasters. That was three times the number affected in the 1970s. Over the same period, economic losses resulting from natural disasters increased five times, from USD 138 billion to USD 629 billion. If current trends continue, the report says, disasters could have a global cost of USD 3,000 billion per decade by the year 2050. Though no country in the world will escape the consequences, it is almost certain that such disasters will mostly end up harming the developing countries with fewest resources to deal with them.

## *Global warming: the facts*

No-one can deny that global warming is occurring, even those who declare that humankind's activities have little or nothing to do with it. Measurements indicate an average global temperature rise of 0.6°C over the past century, with most of that rise taking place during the past few decades. Ten of the warmest years in that period have all occurred since 1990, with 1998 being the warmest year on record, although that record may well be broken in 2006 and broken again before too long.

A number of factors could account for the warming. Solar activity generating more or less short-wave radiation, combined with the trajectory of the Earth around the Sun, certainly has a significant influence on the surface temperature. The combination of these two factors may well be responsible for the Earth slipping in and out of ice ages over the past three million years or so. Yet those factors combined still cannot account for the increasingly rapid warming that is now taking place.

What else is happening? We are emitting large quantities of greenhouse gases as a result of our way of life and the burning of fossil fuels, let alone the destruction of large areas of tropical rain forests. We know too, from the history of climate going back at least half a million years, that changes in the concentrations of

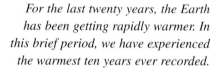

*For the last twenty years, the Earth has been getting rapidly warmer. In this brief period, we have experienced the warmest ten years ever recorded.*

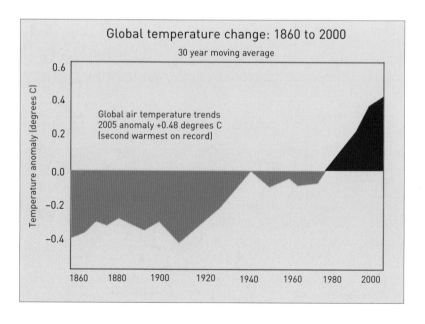

greenhouse gases in the atmosphere, in particular of carbon dioxide and methane, play a considerable role in determining the amount of solar radiation that is retained at the Earth's surface in the form of heat. It makes sense, and is certainly the opinion on scientific grounds of the great majority of climatologists, that it is those emissions, plus changes to the planet's ecosystems that are responsible for heating up the Earth's surface.

Before the Industrial Revolution in the late eighteenth century, the atmosphere had some 280 parts per million (ppm, by volume) of carbon dioxide ($CO_2$). We have now pushed levels up by 30 percent to 380ppm, which, once our models incorporate factors such as the cooling effect of sulphur dioxide emissions from burning coal into, correlates well with the warming of 0.6°C.

In 2006, a research team from Bristol University took data from more than fifty climate models to show the impact of greenhouse gas emissions projected over the coming two centuries, in order to establish what would represent harmful levels of global warming. Their study, published in the *Proceedings of the National Academy of Sciences,* found that an average global temperature increase of no more than 3°C (5.4°F) could result in the soil's store of naturally absorbed carbon being released into the atmosphere, exacerbating the problem of global warming. Rising temperatures would subsequently increase the risk of forest fires, droughts and flooding on a global scale. Areas that would experience the worst forest loss would include Eurasia, eastern China, Canada and the Amazon, while western Africa, southern Europe and eastern US states would be at most risk from dwindling freshwater supplies and droughts. Even if harmful emissions were cut now, many parts of the world would still face a greater risk of natural disasters, the study concluded. It follows that the option of doing nothing, of fiddling while the planet burns, is simply not on offer.

## Gaia and life on earth

The Earth's climate is not something just dumped on the planet to which life has to adapt or be damned. More than forty years ago, the scientist James Lovelock proposed in his famous Gaia Hypothesis that life itself helps to regulate planetary processes, maintaining conditions that continue in turn to support life in all its richness. Climate, as Lovelock conceived it, is therefore part of a system in which life plays a gigantic role, not just as a recipient, but as an

active force. Yet, as if climate were somehow detached from life's activities, we in the industrialized world have taken the planet for granted, consuming its resources as if its bounty was unending and all the while ignoring the ecological services that we get for free.

Climatic variations are perfectly acceptable as part of our living on this planet, as long as they are just that. They indicate that the system is accommodating change, coping with variability, keeping tipping points at bay. It is like the physiology of our bodies that enables us to deal with a myriad of challenges every moment of our lives. Our livers can cope with a certain amount of alcohol, our lungs with a measure of pollution, be it cigarette smoke, our bodies with heat or cold, within limits, and, for a time, we can survive on little water. That is the miracle of our bodies, of our physiology. And we must remember that our bodies run quietly in the background, without any conscious effort of management on our part. Heaven help us were we consciously to attempt to manage our own physical metabolism.

How our bodies work, how we remain alive, is indeed mysterious. We all expect death to come at some point, and it is as if, in an abrupt moment, we pass a point of no return and our bodily functions start disintegrating. Undoubtedly, we can precipitate our demise by smoking; by drinking; or through suffering a heatwave such as struck Europe in 2004 and which led to the premature deaths of some fifteen thousand people.

'Points of no return,' 'critical points,' 'tipping points,' call them what you will, they all express the notion of a brink beyond which we fall into the abyss of irreversible climate change. In his 2005 book *The Revenge of Gaia,* James Lovelock has not minced his words in telling us that the health of this planet and our own future as a species is threatened as never before, not just from global warming and rising temperatures, but from our blind disregard for the natural ecosystems of this planet that provide essential services for all life, and not least for ourselves.

Our worry must be whether we are pushing the system — Gaia, if you like — to the point when it flips and now longer provides those conditions that best suited life in its current form. The Earth has suffered massive extinctions in the past, as when an asteroid, probably about the size of Mount Everest, exploded with the force of millions of atomic bombs just off the Yucatan coast in Mexico. That event, some 65 million years ago, put paid to all the dinosaurs save those that evolved into birds. Perhaps the evolution of warm-bloodedness and the fact that they could fly out of danger, contributed to their

*A powerful storm front and sunset combined have created these crimson skies in Swifts Creek, Victoria, Australia [Peter Firus]*

survival. And surely, if birds were such great survivors, it must be doubly worrying that their populations are those now most in crisis as a result of our devastation of their habitats and ecosystems.

We human beings have had a knack of adapting to extremes of different climates, from the bitter icy Arctic, the scorching deserts of Arabia, the Sahara and Kalahari, the high altitude Himalayas and Andes, to the warm, humid tropics of Southeast Asia, Africa and South America. In effect, we have colonized much of the planet and from a million or so humans some sixty thousand years ago, our numbers have rocketed to more than six billion (US thousand million) people today, with the expectation they may reach eight or nine billion before the century is out. And, with our growing numbers we all need a place to live with shelter, adequate food and, not least, fresh drinkable water.

We have not only adapted ourselves to live in specific environments, we have used our ingenuity to modify and adapt those same environments as exclusively as possible for our own use. To a degree all viable organisms do just that, changing the conditions in their immediate vicinity to suit their own survival within the context of a multi-layered, multi-complex ecosystem. Life, in fact, gives each ecosystem its specific characteristics and, even today, despite its environment having been ravaged over the past half century, a biodiverse-rich country such as Colombia can boast at least 350 distinct ecosystems.

But, in contrast to other forms of life which, left to their own evolutionary devices, share primary resources in a complex food chain, human beings have set out wielding ever more brutal technology, the plough for example, chemical sprays, bulldozers and chainsaws, with the prime purpose of simplifying the environment, to the exclusion of other organisms that are considered competitors for food or threats to health — in other words those that we have designated as the pests and weeds, as well as pathogens.

If we want to survive, or rather if we want our children and grandchildren to survive, it is clearly time to take stock and stop our rampaging across the planet, as if we own it. This book is about climate change and the extreme weather threats we face. It is a book about life and how life generates the best conditions for life through a slow evolutionary process that takes hundreds of thousands of years, if not millions, to develop into a system with the capability to regulate and buffer change. In this book we will take a look at some of the major climatic events that the Earth and ourselves, have experienced over recent years, like the devastating hurricanes that hit North America in 2005, the melting of Arctic ice and the opening of the Northwest Passage, the widespread thawing of permafrost regions, and drought over the Amazon Basin. We will then attempt to unravel the processes of climate that gave rise to such events and come to conclusions as to where we stand today and what the future is likely to bring. In essence, this book is about survival or extinction. Hopefully, the choice is still in our hands.

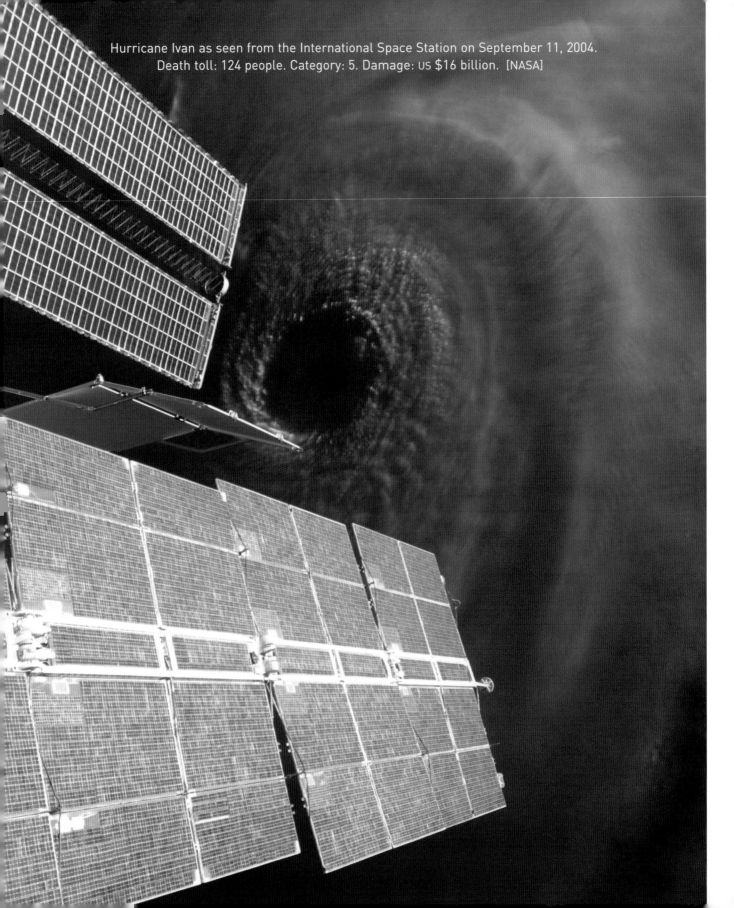

Hurricane Ivan as seen from the International Space Station on September 11, 2004.
Death toll: 124 people. Category: 5. Damage: US $16 billion. [NASA]

# 1. Hurricanes, Tornadoes and Storm Surges

## *Hurricane Katrina*

In the year 2005 came a wake-up call for the United States. Suddenly climate issues mattered and the obduracy of George W. Bush's Administration in denying global warming or — if it was actually happening — that anything needed to be done about it, was no longer proving acceptable to a growing majority of the US population. How did that dramatic change in attitude come about? The simple answer is Hurricane Katrina, which, after striking Louisiana on August 29, 2005, left some 1,500 people dead and many more missing, as well as destruction across four states and a devastated city of New Orleans.

As a top-ranking category 5 hurricane on the Saffir-Simpson scale, with 155 mile per hour winds (250 kilometres per hour), Katrina broke the sea-defence levees protecting the city, which were then swept away in the enormous storm surge of more than 5 metres that followed in the hurricane's wake. The resulting flooding left 80 percent of the city under water, in places as deep as 6

*View of the eyewall of Hurricane Katrina taken on August 28, 2005, as seen from a hurricane hunter aircraft before the storm made landfall on the United States Gulf Coast [NOAA]*

Hurricane Katrina

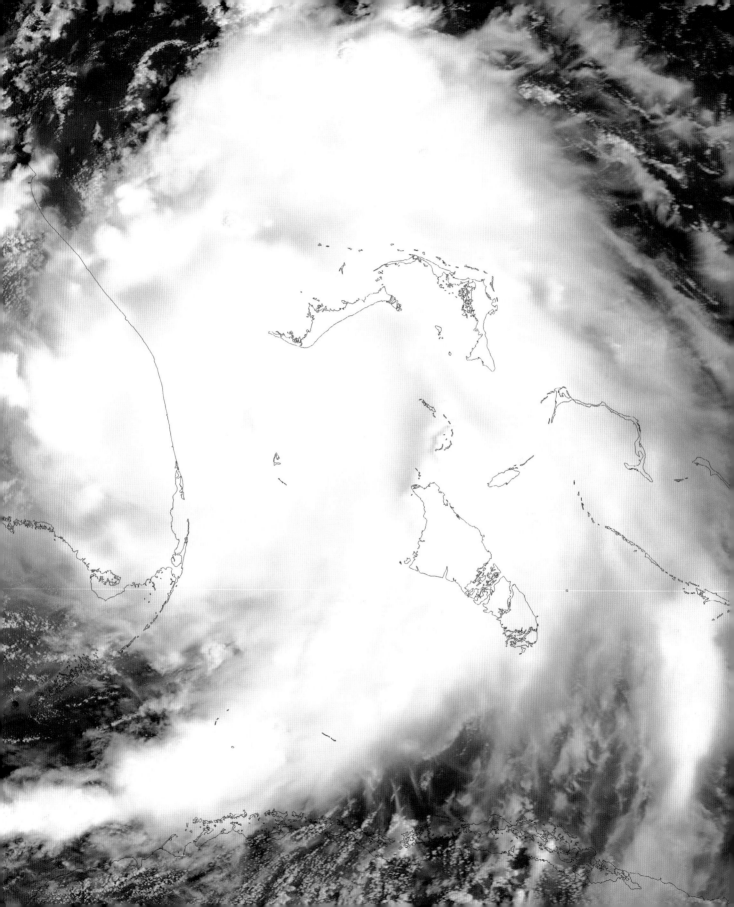

*PREVIOUS PAGE:*
*Hurricane Katrina formed as a tropical depression on late August 23 and developed quickly into a tropical storm by 11 am the next morning. By the time MODIS, NASA's Terra satellite, had captured this picture, Katrina was a category 1 hurricane, approaching the Bahamas and Florida's Atlantic coast with winds of 120 kilometres per hour (75 miles per hour). [NASA]*

*LEFT:*
*August 28, 2005. Hurricane Katrina has gained deadly speed over the warm waters of the Gulf of Mexico with a massive eyewall clearly visible in the middle. At this stage a catebory 5 hurricane, Katrina was set to become one of the most powerful storms to strike the United States, with winds of 257 kilometres per hour (160 miles per hour), causing unprecedented destruction and human suffering. [NASA]*

*BELOW:*
*Floodwaters around the entire downtown New Orleans area after August 29, with the Louisiana Superdome in the centre [U.S. Navy]*

Hurricane Andrew, 1992

*Hurricane Andrew at category 5 strength, and approaching the Bahamas and Miami, Florida, on August 23, 1992  [NOAA]*

*Destruction following Hurricane Andrew, 1992, which was the most destructive hurricane of modern times to affect the United States until Katrina  [NOAA]*

metres. It emerged later that the levees were designed to withstand only category 3 strength hurricanes.

Aside from the known loss of life and the 2,000 or so more who were swept away and disappeared, Katrina left an enormous insurance bill of more than 45 billion US dollars, that surpassed even the destructiveness of Hurricane Andrew of 1992 which, until then, had been the most damaging hurricane of modern times to affect the United States. Added to the ruin of downtown New Orleans and the damage across four states, was the damage at sea to oil rigs and the resulting shutdown and slow recovery in production. According to the review *Business Week* in September 2005, final estimates of overall economic losses caused by Katrina would exceed 200 billion dollars.

*A huge shrimpboat was swept from the sea and about 6 miles inland through the woods on to the side of the road in Long Beach, Mississippi, during Katrina [Scott Carter]*

### Katrina's aftermath

*This wall, located in Gulfport, Mississippi, between Long Beach and Biloxi, is known for withstanding some of the most fierce hurricanes to come through the Mississippi Gulf Coast. In 1947, a Category 2 hurricane came through Gulfport which had a 12 foot surge and left 22 killed. In 1969, Hurricane Camille, a category 5 hurricane, not as massive in size as Katrina but very concentrated, devoured everything in its path: its 22 foot surge killed 137 people and over 8,000 animals. In 2005, Hurricane Katrina ravaged the Mississippi Gulf Coast with category 3/4 winds and a category 5 surge. The ground below this wall is covered in a thick layer of sea shells.*
*[Scott Carter]*

*When the surge comes in, it also goes back out. The débris that the surge contains levels everything it hits and then pulls it back out into the water. People found concrete slabs or holes in the ground where their houses used to be. In many places, the landscape has become completely unrecognizable. Literally nothing is left of the marina in Discovery Bay, Mississippi Gulf Coast (top), where people came to hang out, eat crawfish and oyster, and drink cold beer. The houses that once filled this suburb (right) now lie at the bootom of the bay.* [Scott Carter]

*A picture of a doll swept away and oddly placed by the winds of Katrina* [Thomas Bush]

ABOVE:
*A toxic film spreads over the water near a flooded home in a Lakeside area August 30, 2005, in New Orleans, Louisiana. Estimates put the property loss at nearly $30 billion. About 80 percent of New Orleans was covered by flood waters (see also left, NOAA) as levees broke around Lake Pontchartrain. [Dave Einsel/Getty Images]*

RIGHT:
*New Orleans. View towards Lake Pontchartrain with the flooded Interstate 10. Smoke can be seen rising over the lake from the burning Yacht Club building. [NOAA]*

*Thunder Horse, a semi-submersible platform owned by BP, was found listing after the crew returned. The rig was evacuated for Hurricane Dennis in July 2005. The year 2005 was the most devastating ever to the oil industry of the Gulf of Mexico. A total of 457 pipeline installations and 113 offshore platforms were destroyed.*
*[Robert M. Reed, USCG]*

Oil rigs, pipelines and refineries continued to suffer from the hurricanes that followed in that season, including Rita, Stan and Wilma. Chris Oynes, the regional director of the Mineral Management Service of the United States, estimates that 2005 was the most devastating ever to the oil industry of the Gulf of Mexico. A total of 457 pipeline installations and 113 offshore platforms were destroyed. Recovery has been slow and by the end of May 2006, the production of crude oil, at 324,445 barrels, was down to just 21 percent of its pre-hurricane levels, and natural gas production down to 28 percent. British Petroleum lost its Thunder Horse rig and, as a result, production from all BP sources during the first quarter of 2006, was significantly down, at 4.035 million barrels of oil, from the 4.101 million barrels of the first quarter of 2005. Inevitably the 2005 hurricane season had a strong impact on BP's profits, despite the record rises in the world market prices of petroleum. The overall cost for all the repairs to rigs, pipelines and refineries, not even taking the profits foregone into account, may amount to as much as 31,000 million dollars.

The poorer black people of New Orleans suffered most from Katrina. Not only did they receive insufficient warning of the hurricane's imminent arrival, many were not evacuated in time. Meanwhile, the National Guard did not move into action because of red tape and officials blocked the initial efforts of the Red Cross. Thousands of people were left sheltering but stranded in the Superdome sports stadium after being evacuated from their homes.

Even President George W. Bush displayed a lack of leadership, not even visiting the region until four days after the disaster. When Bush finally showed up, he patted Michael D Brown, the director of the Federal Emergency Management Agency (FEMA) on the back, telling him: 'Brownie, you're doing a heck of a job.' With people still waiting to be rescued from their homes ten days later, Brown resigned. Charity, the city's main hospital since its founding in 1736, was badly damaged. As reported by Karyn Miller in the *Sunday Telegraph* (April 24, 2006), eight months later it was not yet back in service and its medical staff were operating from a military tent erected in a convention centre car park. Dr Peter DeBlieux, the head of the emergency room, could not be more explicit in his frustration that the hospital, as it stands, could treat only one third of the number of patients that it treated prior to Katrina and even then serious cases had to be sent elsewhere. 'This is the United States of America,' he said. 'This is not a Third World Country.'

At the end of May 2006, nine months after the destruction of New Orleans, fewer than 190,000 inhabitants out of 455,000 had returned to New Orleans, and of those who did, the majority were white middle-class citizens, living in areas where the pace of reconstruction was far more rapid than taking place in the predominantly poorer sections of the city. Katrina has given the western world its first experience of 'environmental refugees' on a major scale. It is an event which is likely to be repeated if our climate really does begin to break down.

But 2005 wasn't just Katrina. That year broke all-time records for tropical storms and hurricanes arising out of the Atlantic Ocean. A total of twenty-eight severe tropical storms and fifteen hurricanes, seven of which were in the higher categories and three (Katrina, Rita and Wilma) in category 5, were recorded between June 1 and November 30. And Spain and Portugal had their first-ever recorded hurricane, Vince, which struck off the west coast of the Iberian peninsula on July 15 that year. Hurricane Vince started as a tropical storm between the Azores and the Canaries in unusually cool waters for hurricane formation, 23°C rather than the 26°C normally required.

Nevertheless, in its traverse in a north-easterly direction, it acquired the deep convection and tropical characteristics of a hurricane.

The year before, on March 26, 2004, the South Atlantic was surprised by its first-ever recorded hurricane, Catarina, with 150 kilometres per hour winds coming ashore in the southern Brazilian state of Santa Catarina, causing considerable damage and some loss of life, and leaving 33,000 homeless. Hurricanes are not supposed to happen in that part of the world, and Catarina attracted scarcely any international media attention.

By way of comparison, one of the most powerful hurricanes ever observed, Hurricane Mitch, with winds of up to 180 kilometres per hour, struck Central America in the autumn of 1998, killing as many as 20,000 people. Millions were left homeless in Honduras, Nicaragua, El Salvador and Guatemala, mostly as a result of horrendous mudslides slipping down slopes that had been shorn of their trees. Hurricane Mitch caused several billion dollars worth of damage. Had a hurricane of that devastating force struck the United States the cost would have been many times more, and no doubt the television and newspaper coverage proportionally higher.

*The citizens of Tegucigalpa, Honduras, return to their homes badly damaged by Hurricane Mitch, 1998 [PAP]*

The statistics speak for themselves. According to research which appeared in the journal *Science* (September 16, 2005), the average annual number of Category 4 and 5 hurricanes worldwide nearly doubled over the past thirty-five years. A contributing cause is the fact that global sea-surface temperatures have increased over the same period.

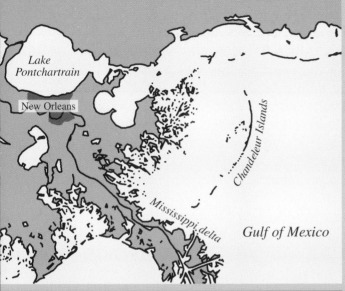

## Chandeleur Islands

*Katrina's relentless winds and waves caused dramatic changes to the US Gulf Coast. The gracefully curved Chandeleur Islands form a protective wall between the open sea of the Gulf of Mexico and the Mississippi delta, sheltering the mainland during storms. In the eleven months between October 14, 2004 (see below left), and September 16, 2005, when the right-hand image was taken, the islands have almost been washed away. [NASA]*

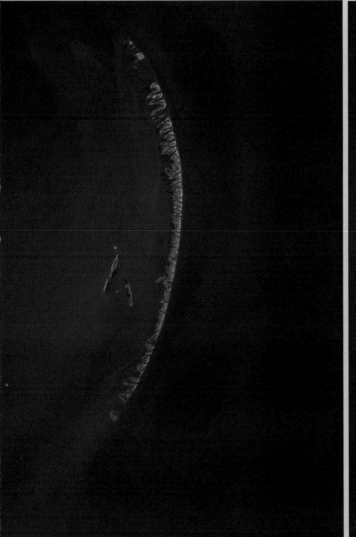

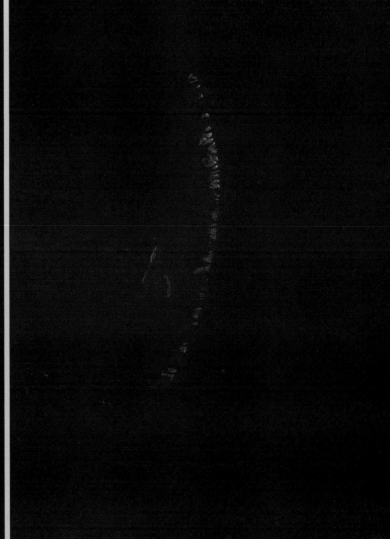

## Hurricane categories

The way storm surge, wind and other factors combine determines the destructive power of a hurricane. The National Oceanic and Atmospheric Administration uses a scale which assigns storms to five categories. This can be used to estimate the potential property damage and flooding expected along the hurricane's path.

The scale was formulated in 1969 by Herbert Saffir, a consulting engineer, and Dr Bob Simpson, director of the National Hurricane Center. The World Meteorological Organization was preparing a report on structural damage to dwellings due

*A girl playing with a cardboard box outside her family's makeshift home in Tegucigalpa, Honduras. Many people lost their homes in the murderous floods brought by Hurricane Mitch and had to rebuilt them from scrap metal and driftwood recovered from the banks of the nearby Choluteca River.  [Orlando Sierra, PAP]*

to windstorms, and Dr Simpson added information
about storm surge heights that accompany hurricanes in each category.

| CATEGORY | WINDS | EFFECTS |
|---|---|---|
| One | 74–95 mph | No real damage to building structures. Damage primarly to unanchored mobile homes, shrubbery, and trees. Also, some coastal road flooding and minor pier damage. |
| Two | 96–110 mph | Some roofing material, door, and window damage to buildings. Considerable damage to vegetation, mobile homes, and piers. Coastal and low-lying escape routes flood 2–4 hours before arrival of center. Small craft in unprotected anchorages break moorings. |
| Three | 111–130 mph | Some structural damage to small residences and utility buildings with a minor amount of curtainwall failures. Mobile homes are destroyed. Flooding near the coast destroys smaller structures with larger structures damaged by floating débris. Terrain continuously lower than 5 feet ASL (above sea level) may be flooded inland 8 miles or more. |
| Four | 131–155 mph | More extensive curtainwall failures with some complete roof strucutre failure on small residences. Major erosion of beach. Major damage to lower floors of structures near the shore. Terrain continuously lower than 10 feet ASL may be flooded requiring massive evacuation of residential areas inland as far as 6 miles. |
| Five | greater than 155 mph | Complete roof failure on many residences and industrial buildings. Some complete building failures with small utility buildings blown over or away. Major damage to lower floors of all structures located less than 15 feet ASL and within 500 yards of the shoreline. Massive evacuation of residential areas on low ground within 5 to 10 miles of the shoreline may be required. |

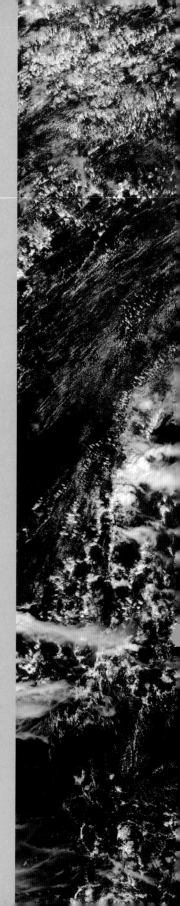

OPPOSITE:
*Cyclone Adeline-Juliet as a
beautifully symmetric swirl
of clouds on April 9, 2005,
captured by the MODIS
(Moderate Resolution Imaging
Spectroradiometer) on NASA's
Aqua satellite. In the centre
is a well-formed eye, through
which the dark waters of the
Indian Ocean are clearly visible. Adeline-Juliet degraded
after this image was taken,
and by April 12, was no longer
a cyclone-strength storm. The
storm never threatened any
landmass. [NASA]*

## The naming of hurricanes

For centuries, major storms have attracted names
which in some cases became legendary for their
strength and violence. The Spanish custom from the
sixteenth century was to name Atlantic storms after
the saint's day on which they made landfall, like
Hurricane San Felipe which struck Puerto Rico in
1876. In 1928, by coincidence the very same saint's
day, September 13, saw the arrival of San Felipe
Segundo (known better in Florida as Hurricane
Okeechobee for the storm surge it caused from the
lake of that name) which was the only Category 5
hurricane ever to hit Puerto Rico.

As time went on, other informal naming strategies included army and navy personnel's pet names
for their girlfriends or wives, as well as the standard
radio phonetic alphabet. Latitude and longitude were
used more formally, but this style was too confusing
for general public use as storms constantly shifted
position.

So around 1950, the US Weather Bureau began
to assign female first names, in alphabetical order,
with alternating male names being added later as
a gesture to changing political correctness. In the
system that has now emerged in use with the World
Meteorological Organization, each region around
the world has its own list of names. In the case of
Atlantic storms, six lists of twenty-one names are
rotated year by year, each name coming up in alphabetical order, though names that begin with Q, U, X,
Y and Z are always excluded from use. Should the
number of hurricanes in any one year exceed the list
of names, then the designations Alpha, Beta, Gamma,
and so on, using the Greek alphabet, come into play.

And speaking of legends, the names of storms that
acquire fame for their strength and violence, such as
Gloria (1985), Bob (1991), Andrew (1992), and Rita
(2005), are simply removed from the list and never
used again. The list of 'retired' names is long. It goes
without saying that we shall never again see another
Hurricane Katrina.

## What causes hurricanes?

It is tempting to ascribe such extreme events as Hurricane Mitch and Katrina to changes in climate and therefore to greenhouse gas emissions and global warming. A confounding factor, says Kerry Emanuel of Massachusetts Institute of Technology, is a natural cycle in which some decades are more active than others, because of oscillating circulation changes in the North Atlantic. Meteorologists have determined that the 1930s, 40s and 50s were periods of strong cyclonic activity in the Northern Atlantic and the 1960s until the 1980s more tranquil. Since 1995, hurricanes have been getting stronger and more numerous.

When taking into account the warming of tropical waters, the energy content of hurricanes has gone up far more than predicted. Meteorologists had predicted a 10 percent increase in wind speeds for every 1°C rise in surface water temperatures in the tropical Atlantic. Instead, says Emanuel in a report published in *Nature* (July 2005), 'Our predictions were way off. Wind speeds have risen by up to 80 percent.'

Like tropical rainforests, hurricanes export heat to the higher latitudes and therefore the more category 5 hurricanes that are spawned the greater the transport of energy out of the tropical system and into the temperate zones. That might help even out some of the consequences of global warming.

Thunderstorms, a warm tropical ocean and the spin of the Earth — the Coriolis Force — are the basic ingredients for cyclones to start swirling around a central axis, known as the 'eye' of the storm, and to generate hurricanes in the northern Atlantic ocean (or typhoons in the Pacific). In forming a thunderstorm, the air, now laden with water vapour from the sea surface, rises upwards, drawing in more air to replace it via the trade winds that are blowing across the sea surface from Africa. As the air rises it cools, water vapour condenses, and the latent heat inherent in turning liquid water into vapour, is again released, so fuelling the convection process. As a result the air within the cyclone can rise virtually to the top of the troposphere — the lower atmosphere — attaining heights of 10,000 metres (33,000 feet) above the ocean surface, where the air is too cold for the convection process to proceed any higher.

Once the air has risen as far as it can go, it spins ever outwards from the eye, producing the telltale bank of deep cirrus clouds. Whereas the air rising in the convection process moves in anti-clockwise direction, the air spinning out from the hurricane moves in the opposite

direction, and sinks back to the ocean surface, where, depending on the size and strength of the hurricane, it may get drawn again into the 'eye.' The energy of the sun therefore initially drives the process, but only inasmuch it can bring about sufficient water evaporation, which like coal burning in a furnace, is the actual fuel.

Hurricanes vary considerably in size and strength, which gives them the categories of 1 to 5. The lowest categories may stretch over 100 kilometres and the higher categories over 1,500 kilometres and therefore fifteen times more. Mind-boggling energies are involved in the formation and sustaining of a hurricane. Every second of its existence, a large hurricane requires the energy-equivalent of an atomic bomb going off every second. Just one hurricane consumes the equivalent amount of energy to fuel the United States for a hundred years, all in the form of condensing water vapour and the right speed of spin of the earth.

Once the hurricane reaches land, it loses its source of energy in the form of water vapour and transforms into a tropical storm that over the space of several days will literally run out of steam.

*Damage caused by Hurricane Dennis at Navarre Beach, Florida, in July 2005 [FEMA]*

## What dying coral reefs tell us

'If you want to see a coral reef, go now, because they just won't survive in their current state.' This dire warning came from biochemistry professor M. James Crabbe of the University of Luton in the UK. In a report by AP science writer Seth Borenstein ('Caribbean coral suffers record death,' March 30, 2006) he was commenting on the high mortality rate of coral reefs being registered around the world, from the Caribbean to the Indian Ocean.

Routine monitoring reveals that reefs in Puerto Rico and the US Virgin Islands are currently showing a 30 percent loss of living coral in reefs which are hundreds of years old, a loss that these slow-growing reefs can never recover from. Entire colonies of brain coral have been lost, according to Edwin Hernandez-Delgado, a University of Puerto Rico biology researcher, a phenomenon which has never been observed before. In some places, brain coral is 90 percent dead from the disease called 'white plague,' which arises when hot sea temperatures kill off the algae on which the coral reefs are nourished. When the algae die, they turn white, and the bleached coral quickly dies off unless the situation is reversed. Usually some bleaching occurs in patches where the water temperature may be higher, but in 2005,

*A closeup of a cavernous star coral* (Montastrea cavernosa) *[NOAA]*

*A dead coral reef [NOAA]*

bleaching occurred across a wide region, and at all depths, following a critical rise in sea temperatures over a long period. Researchers say that the 2005 sea 'heatwave' was the worst in twenty years of monitoring, and actually bigger than the previous twenty years combined.

'This is probably a harbinger of things to come,' said John Rollino, the chief scientist for the Bahamian Reef Survey. 'The coral bleaching is probably more a symptom of disease — the widespread global environmental degradation — that's going on.'

According to Professor Crabbe, the evidence of global warming is overwhelming. 'The prognosis is not good,' he said. 'The big problem for coral is the question of whether they can adapt sufficiently quickly to cope with climate change. ... I think the evidence we have at the moment is: No, they can't.'

## Tornadoes

Tornadoes, tropical storms, blizzards and polar-front storms all, in their different way, depend on the characteristics of water vapour as a transporter of latent energy. On condensing, that latent energy is released, either in the form of generating tropical thunderstorms or in the clashing of warm and cold fronts, which give rise to stormy conditions.

Some one thousand tornadoes, with their characteristic snaking, twisting column of air funnelling down from the storm clouds above, strike the United States every year. A small proportion of those 'twisters' are truly dangerous and, where they touch down, they can kill, as well as flattening buildings, throwing cars around, snapping trees in half and bringing down power lines. Within the

*OPPOSITE:*
*An approaching tornado*
*[Paul & Lindamarie Ambrose,*
*Getty Images]*

*BELOW:*
*This series shows how gradually more dust and débris is sucked higher into the clouds as the tornado wins in strength [NOAA]*

Tornado damage in Lancaster, Texas
[David W. Hamilton, Getty Images]

tornado wind speeds may reach more than 500 kilometres per hour, giving the twister incredible powers. Meanwhile, the erratic movement and the speed while traversing the ground, sometimes as fast as a speeding car, can make it virtually impossible to predict precisely the path of a tornado.

In 1925, on March 18, the Tri-State tornado charged its way across Missouri, Illinois and Indiana, killing 695 people and injuring 2,000. Nearly fifty years later, on April 3, 1974, on 'Terrible Tuesday' a total of 148 tornadoes were spawned over a 24-hour period, passing across twelve states from Michigan and Alabama,

*Waterspouts are a common sight over warm waters anywhere around the world but especially in tropical latitudes. They form like short-lived tornadoes under heavy cloud, drawing up water vapour in their vortex, and can be up to a mile or more in height and hundreds of feet wide. Large waterspouts can be extremely dangerous for boats at sea. Here we see a slender waterspout on the Mediterranean coast at Terracina in Lazio, Italy.  [MM, Wikipedia]*

leaving 309 dead and 5,300 injured, with damages amounting to 600 million US dollars in the money of the time. Then twenty-five years later, the United States was subjected to its fiercest tornadoes ever, when forty separate twisters killed forty-three people and injured seven hundred. One tornado struck Oklahoma City, leaving a wake of destruction one kilometre wide, with 1,800 homes totally destroyed and another 2,500 damaged. The cost in damages then amounted to 1,200 million US dollars.

Tornadoes are by no means limited to the United States. They occur in Europe, including the UK, where slates can be lifted of roofs and windows sucked out and they occur in Australia, Japan and Central Asia. Tornadoes are mini-hurricanes in the sense that some of the same conditions have to be met, but because they form over land rather than over the warm tropical ocean, they do not have the same opportunities to draw into the 'eye' an almost inexhaustible supply of energy in the form of warm, tropical, surface waters. Tornadoes result from warm, humid air from the ground meeting cold, dry air above, with the result that massive cumulonimbus thunderstorm clouds form. The larger the storm clouds, the more humid air from the ground gets sucked up. The spinning of the air, such that a funnel forms, depends, as with hurricanes, on both the Coriolis Force, and on the jet stream above. If the latter catches an edge of the storm that adds to the spin, sending the outer layers of the storm swirling in cyclonic fashion. Air flows outwards from the top of the funnel and down at the edges of the storm. Meanwhile, warm, humid air from the ground is drawn upwards into the storm clouds, fuelling the spin and sustaining the funnel, until the process, like a hurricane passing over land, runs out of steam.

## The El Niño phenomenon

The El Niño phenomenon (more technically known as ENSO — the El Niño Southern Oscillation) in the tropical Pacific Ocean, in which the winds and currents blow towards the South American coast rather than towards South East Asia and Australia, tends to dampen tropical storm and hurricane activity in the northern hemisphere tropical Atlantic.

The flow of tropical Pacific Ocean waters either to the west or to the east has a profound impact on the world's weather, causing flooding where there was drought and dry conditions where normally monsoons occur. During the course of 1997 and lasting into 1998, the world experienced one of the most powerful El Niño events of the twentieth century, and the fundamental change that it caused in the world's weather, resulted in billions of dollars of damage and as many as 23,000 deaths. During that event, Australia and Indonesia among other countries, suffered a drawn-out drought and devastating forest fires. Deforestation in Indonesia because of logging and the substitution of forest by plantations of African palm, allowed the fires to spread underground to where peat had accumulated over millions of years. In places those fires are still burning, helped on by further deforestation.

Most years the trade winds blow across the Pacific Ocean from east to west, driving the surface waters with them, such that they pile up against the eastern coasts of Indonesia and Australia. Those years when the effect is particularly strong are known as 'La Niña' years. The strong upwards convection over the north eastern part of Australia and over Indonesia leads to a healthy monsoon season and, as part of the workings of La Niña, the westwards movement of the surface waters draws in the cold, nutrient rich waters flowing northwards from Antarctica. The resulting current of water, the Humboldt Current, surfaces off the coast of Peru, fertilizing the ocean and making those coastal waters some of the richest fisheries in the world. In fact, the mountains of guano, or accumulated bird droppings, indicate just how much seabirds have benefited from the bounties brought in from Antarctica. La Niña also generates one of the driest deserts in the world, Chile's Atacama Desert, and allows the trade winds to blow freely across the Atlantic Ocean, so bringing monsoon conditions to Amazonia. Both hurricanes in the Atlantic and typhoons in the Pacific tend to be more prevalent, longer lasting and stronger during La Niña years.

What a contrast in the case of El Niño years! Then the currents in the Pacific Ocean reverse, such as to flow from Asia towards South America, and instead of taking place over the land mass to the west, the large updraughts of the convective process occur over mid-ocean. In reaching the west coast of South America, the surface waters of the tropical Pacific suppress the Humboldt Current, leading to a crash in the anchovy industry. Not only are the trade winds of the Pacific Ocean suppressed during an El Niño event, but also those of the Atlantic. That has an impact on the flow of air and the convective process over the Amazon Basin.

Were one El Niño to follow another in quick succession, the rainforests of the central Amazon Basin would be put under considerable stress, even to the point of disappearing, at least in their current form. In that respect the predictions of the UK Met Office Hadley Centre, from models that have been elaborated to take plant physiology into account, indicate that continued global warming could lead to a succession of El Niño-like events. Three successive years of strong El Niños, with the resulting suppression of the Atlantic trade winds, would play havoc with global climate, affecting not just the Basin, but the monsoons over India and south east Asia.

In contrast to 2005, the year 2006 is an El Niño year. The total number of hurricanes and tropical storms during the June 1 to November 30 season are expected to amount to seventeen, of which five could reach hurricane status, with winds and storm surges putting them into categories of 3 to 5. Meanwhile, in the Pacific Ocean, of the eleven anticipated tropical storms, two could reach typhoon or cyclone status in categories of 3 to 5. One, in fact, already happened. On March 20, 2006, Queensland in Australia was hit by the biggest cyclone for decades, leaving thousands homeless, as their houses collapsed around them in tropical storm winds that reached nearly 300 kilometres per hour. Miraculously, no-one was killed.

## Polar front storm surges

It is hardly surprising that we should be so obsessed with the weather in the UK. Britain happens to be in the path of clashing atmospheric fronts and the result is unpredictable weather, the nightmare and challenge for meteorologists. In the United Kingdom we are situated between a maritime north-westerly that brings cool, gale-force winds from northern Canada and the Arctic Ocean; a northerly wind, the Arctic maritime, which, if it prevails, can bring bitter cold; the polar continental from the north east, with its blasts of chill winds from Siberia, often the harbinger of heavy snow-storms; the south-westerlies, associated with the Gulf Stream and, at least for western Britain, the prevailing winds that bring warm, wet weather; and finally winds from the South that are associated with heatwaves such as the one experienced during July of 2006.

Polar front storms can bring winter squalls, snowfalls and blizzards. They are usually sudden, and result from cold polar air shifting southwards and encountering the warmer air moving up from the tropics. Air masses, like rivers flowing one into the other, tend to stick to their own, with little initial mixing. Warmer air that originates from the tropics carries moisture with it in contrast to the dry, colder more dense air of the Arctic, or Antarctic. In general, the polar front arises when the tropical maritime air is forced up and over the northerly air, leaving behind a region of deep low pressure, therefore a 'depression.' As the warm air gets pushed up it cools and releases its water vapour in the form of showers of rain.

The encounter between the air masses forces changes in the jet streams of air that flow in anti-clockwise direction around the Arctic. Where the warm, moister air has the advantage it pushes the jet stream further north, and vice versa, when the Arctic air has the edge it pushes southwards. The net result is that the jet stream encircles and finally cuts off large cells of polar and tropical air. When the tropical air mass has gained the upper hand and pushed northwards, cyclones form at the boundaries and vice versa anti-cyclones when the Arctic air has forced its way southwards.

Polar front storms can wreak considerable damage. Storm surges caused by deep depressions, heavy rainfall over land, and strong winds coinciding with high tides can be fatal. They are not necessarily associated with global warming and some of the more violent incidents in Europe took place during the Little Ice Age of the late medieval period. Between 1240 and 1362, sixty parishes in the province of Schleswig in Denmark were swallowed by the sea and a third of a million people drowned, a massive number when one takes the size of population into account. At that time, the island of Heligoland in the German Bight was so eroded by storms and sea-surges that from being 60 kilometres across in the year 800 it now measures no more than 1.5 kilometres at its widest point.

Devastating storms have continued to batter coasts around the North Sea throughout history, causing severe erosion of the land in areas like East Anglia. In August 1413 a southerly storm struck the east coast of Scotland and wiped out the town of Forvie in Aberdeenshire. Today, all that can be seen of the medieval town is a thirty-metre high sand dune.

In medieval times, some attempts were made to erect barriers to prevent storm surges bringing sea-water inland, the most ambitious being the dykes and other structures built in the Netherlands to keep the sea at bay, but in the worst of storms even they were grossly inadequate. In 1953, a terrible combination of tides, storm winds and sea-surge in the North Sea left hundreds dead in northern Europe, not least in the region around the Thames estuary where some three hundred people were drowned. In the low-lying

Netherlands, of which over a quarter of the land area is below sea-level, 1,800 people lost their lives.

The problem that Londoners and others around the Thames estuary face with regard to storm surges is twofold: first rising sea-levels and potentially stormier conditions as global warming gets into its stride; and second that London is sinking and has sunk by a metre since Samuel Pepys recorded a serious flooding of central London in the late seventeenth century. Then Westminster was left with water slopping some 6 feet high, and London continued to be vulnerable to flooding.

That 1953 disaster spurred the idea of the Thames Barrier, the work being completed by 1982. When shut, the massive gates can prevent a storm surge from causing flooding all the way to the centre of London. The barrier, as it stands, spans the 520 metre wide stretch known as Woolwich reach and consists of ten moveable gates. Since its completion, the Barrier has been raised many times, at times as a precaution, but mainly for regular testing and maintenance. It was designed to serve its purpose at least until 2030, based on projections of higher tidal levels which are calculated to rise at a rate of about 60 centimetres per century. More recently, a vastly more ambitious plan has been proposed for a ten-mile long barrier extending right across the Thames estuary from Essex to Kent.

Facing a similar threat across the North Sea, the Netherlands' experience of disastrous flooding goes back for centuries, but the major sea-defences were built in the twentieth century, such as the Afsluitdijk dam which dates from 1932 and was built in response to a disastrous flooding in 1916. Similarly, the terrible floods of 1953 led to the development of the country's huge Delta project, generating a system of dykes and gates that culminated in the construction of the Oosterscheldedam.

However, the Netherlands now faces a longer-term threat on a considerable scale, as the latest projections of rising sea-levels due to climate change provoke much thought as to how sustainable are some of the more recent sea-walls. Recent studies, based on the most modest projections, expect the sea-level to rise by 20 to 110 centimetres by 2100, on average, as we have seen, by 60 centimetres. Thus, in the future, stronger dykes and sea-defences will surely be needed. Without countermeasures, the threats of floods will be significantly higher. One proposal is that some areas taken from the sea may now be given back, in an attempt to relieve flood pressure. In a similar move recently, a large area of reclaimed wetland in eastern England was similarly returned to its previous tidal flooding, in a move designed both to restore natural habitats and to ease flooding pressure elsewhere along the east coast. Assessments by the Environmental Studies Department of the Vrije Universiteit in Amsterdam suggest, given a worst-case scenario of a projected rise of 5 metres in sea-level over the next century, which takes global warming factors into account, that there is a high probability of parts of the south west and north west of the Netherlands simply being abandoned.

But the scale of flooding around the North Sea from storm surges pales into insignificance when measured against the impact of a storm surge on Bangladesh during heavy monsoon rains (see Chapter 4). The sheer enormity of the task of trying to keep the sea out of this low-lying land is enough to daunt the most adventurous of engineers. Furthermore, a large sector of the Bangladesh population relies on its rivers, such as the Ganges, flowing freely into the sea and bringing with them millions of tonnes of nutrient rich sediments that make the river plains and estuary one of the most fertile soils in the world, but at a high price.

## Blizzards

Blizzards are undoubtedly the worst of winter storms. Strong winds, snow that blows horizontally, ice storms that bring down power lines and crush roofs, and finally avalanches, are well known phenomena in the higher latitudes. North America, just as it suffers most from tornadoes, is home to the worst blizzards imaginable, with masses of snow falling in a very short time and even covering trains that have been caught up in the storm.

In the year 1888 two devastating blizzards struck the United States, the first paralyzing the northeastern part of the country and leaving four hundred people dead, two hundred ships sunk and snowdrifts that reached a height of 50 feet (15 metres) in some areas. The same year the Great Plains were hit by a savage blizzard that killed 235 people and left children trapped in their schools.

The United States confers the term 'blizzard' to snowstorms in which visibility is reduced to less than 400 metres for three consecutive hours, which precipitate snow or ice and which have wind speeds of at least 35 miles per hour (56 kilometres per hour) and therefore 7 or more on the Beaufort Wind Scale. Canada has a slightly modified definition of blizzard. The winds must be blowing

at a minimum speed of 40 kilometres per hour and visibility down to less than 1 kilometre. The storm must last at least four hours and have a wind chill factor of less than –25°C. A 'whiteout' is the most difficult weather event to cope with. For anyone caught out in such a storm it becomes well nigh impossible to distinguish the ground from the air, leading to complete disorientation.

The problem is that the extreme weather conditions that result in blizzards are hard to predict, since they require a sudden juxtaposition between two fronts, the one polar in its origins and the other warm, humid and semi-tropical. The forcing up of the warm front over the colder, drier front, generates turbulent conditions, with the release of much of the water vapour contained in the original warm front.

The suddenness and unpredictability of such storms can catch people off their guard and they may find themselves exposed to bitter temperatures, after basking in the warmth of the warm front. The

*A woman walks through a snow covered alley in January 2005 in Tsunanmachi, Japan. A record snowfall accumulated 360 cm of snow and killed about 100 people across Japan. [Koichi Kamoshida/Getty Images]*

*Record snowfall in Bavaria, January 2006*
*[Christoph Kurtzmann]*

## Collapse

These pictures remind us just how
vulnerable our human structures
and infrastructures are to extreme
weather events. We have come
to depend completely on roads,
buildings and power-grids for our
safety and convenience, but all of
these can fail dramatically in the
face of natural forces. At the same
time, natural structures such as
trees adapt on the whole to specific
environments in which they survive
all but the severest conditions.

ABOVE:
*Broken high tension pylons near Münster, Germany, November 2005. In the Münster region as many as fifty high tension pylons were either broken or no longer functional after heavy snowfalls. About 65,000 people were left without electricity and heating.*
[Franz Peter Tschauner, PAP]

FAR LEFT:
*Rescue workers searching for victims at the collapsed skating rink in Bad Reichenhall, Germany, January 2006. Fifteen people died after the roof of the skating rink caved in under the pressure of heavy snow.* [PAP]

LEFT:
*Driving through a blizzard* [Helmut Gevert]

Armistice Day Blizzard in 1940 is a classic example. In the morning the temperature was a relatively balmy 15°C for the time of the year, but by noon it was snowing heavily. Altogether, 154 people died, some from being caught outside and others trapped in their cars.

One of the worst blizzards of the past thirty years was the blizzard of 1978, which formed after three air masses merged into one, and converged over New England. A stationary high-pressure zone over eastern Canada effectively trapped the blizzard south of the New England coast, causing bands of snow to sweep continuously over the same area. Wind speeds reached near-hurricane levels of over 100 kilometres per hour and the air mass even took on the appearance of a hurricane with an 'eye' located in the middle.

Many people were caught in the storm while driving, others were trapped in their homes or offices with snowdrifts of more than 2 metres deep, that blocked exits. Meanwhile, storm force winds caused sea-surges with resulting flooding along coastal areas. Several thousand homes were destroyed, roads had to be shut down and a number of people died in trying to find shelter. A week after the storm had abated, people were still left without heat, water, food, and electricity. Approximately ten thousand people had to be moved into emergency shelters. Even with the help of the United States National Guard it took almost a week to clear the roads, as a result of buried cars and trucks that needed to be removed; some side streets, such as Dunster Road, in Boston's Jamaica Plain were so heavily piled with snow that they could not be cleared until the snow melted months later.

However, on March 12, 1993, the 'Storm of the Century' struck the US, with snow conditions stretching over twenty-six states, reaching as far north as Canada and all the way down to Mexico. In southern states, such as parts of Alabama, more snow fell during the storm that had ever fallen in an entire winter. Power was cut, highways and airports had to be closed, and to add insult to injury fifteen tornadoes sprang into action in Florida. By the time the Storm of the Century was over, it had caused the death of 270 people inland, with 48 others reported missing at sea.

But blizzards are not confined to the North American continent, and during February 1999 the European Alps suffered from one of the heaviest snowfalls in living memory, leaving as many as seventy people dead and tens of thousands of ski enthusiasts stranded. Some 38 people died in the villages of Galtur and Valzur, close to Innsbruck in the Austrian Alps, as a result of the heavy snows culminating in avalanches.

*People are having fun in the snow in Segovia, Spain, in February
2006. Most of the country was covered in white after heavy snowfall.*
*[Juan Martin, PAP]*

*A rare site: snow covering the Acropolis in Athens, Greece, in February 2004*
*[Louisa Gouliamaki, PAP]*

The winter of 2005–6 produced extreme cold and snow conditions across a wide swathe of European countries, from Russia to Greece. In Poland, the sheer weight of snow apparently caused a trade centre to collapse in Katowice, killing at least sixty-five people. Some five hundred people were in the hall for an exhibition when the roof caved in. Among the dead and some 140 injured were Poles, Belgians and Germans. In Greece that same January, more than four hundred villages and towns were cut off after thirty-six hours of continuous snowfall.

Equally, the winter of 2005–6 saw Japan's heaviest snowfalls for more than twenty years and the highest on record, causing over one hundred fatalities and thousands of injuries. In places up to 3 metres of snow piled up, causing buildings to collapse. Niigata and Nagano prefectures, north-west of Tokyo, were among the hardest hit. Main highways were closed and many mountain communities completely cut off.

While none of these events is conclusive in itself, certainly it seems the year 2005 wanted to leave its severe weather stamp across the globe, as the following winter was one of the bitterest on record, with Arctic conditions sweeping across the European continent. February 2006 similarly brought blizzard conditions to America's East Coast, from New England down to Maryland, including New York, where 27 inches of snow in Central Park broke a record of 26.4 inches set in December 1947, according to the National Weather Service. Lightning and thunder accompanied some of the snowfall, a rare phenomenon dubbed 'thundersnow' by the Weather Service.

*Japanese Macaque monkeys endured unseasonably cold and snowy weather in the mountains of Nagano province in central Japan in January 2006. Macaques have become extremely adapted to their surroundings, soaking in hot springs during the harsh winter months. Young Macaques even enjoy rolling snowballs, much like human children.*
*[Shusuke Sezai, PAP]*

## 2. Heatwaves and Drought

OPPOSITE:
[David Ritter]

In late July 2003, a heatwave that lasted for days took temperatures close to 40°C over southern Europe, causing crops to wilt and rivers to fall to dangerously low levels. France with its high dependence on nuclear power stations to provide electricity — more than 75 percent — had to shut down reactors to avoid 'thermal pollution' of those rivers that, like the Loire, provide cooling water to condense the steam generated for the running of the turbines. But there was to be a more dramatic and worrying consequence in France which gave great cause for concern.

The unprecedented high temperatures killed some three thousand people from heat exhaustion and dehydration, which led the health minister, Jean-François Mattei, to pronounce that France had

*Patients are being treated during the heatwave that hit France in August 2003, at Saint-Antoine hospital in Paris. France's health ministry said that up to 3,000 people may have died across the country from a two-week heatwave that scorched much of Europe, confirming the toll put forward by doctors who had accused the government of underestimating the scale of the disaster.*
*[Jean Ayissi, Getty Images]*

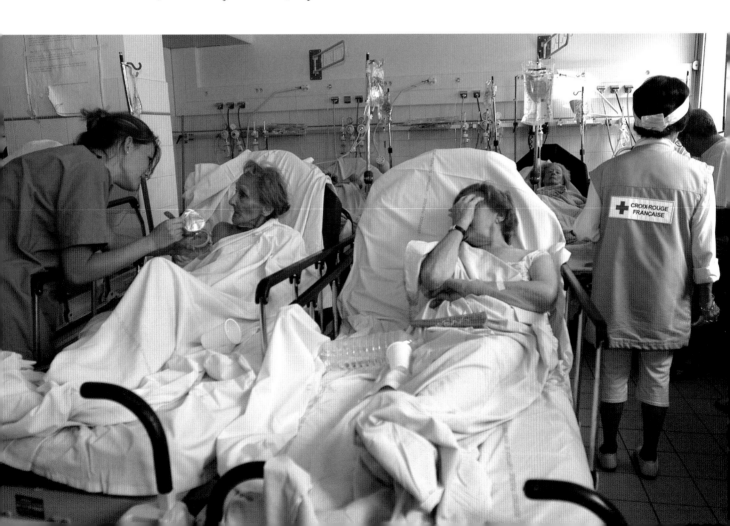

*Members of the Civil Defence service stand on a road next to a pine grove in the village of Conil de la Frontera, Cadiz, southern Spain, where forest fires broke out in July 2006. Many people had to be evacuated from their homes as fires were getting closer and closer to residential areas.*
*[Jorge Zapata, PAP]*

suffered a 'veritable epidemic of deaths.' General Funeral Services, France's largest undertaker, handled some 3,230 deaths from August 4 to 10 compared to 2,300 on an average week in the year, a 40 percent jump. Over the period of the summer, a total of 15,000 people were estimated to have died. The fact that many of them were old people who appeared to have suffered because families were away on holiday, sat heavily on the nation's conscience.

Nor did the summer of 2006 prove very different in heatwave terms. Temperatures well above 30°C (86°F) were registered across Europe during a large part of July, on one occasion exceeding 35°C in parts of the UK. With memories still vivid of the 2003 summer, France's health minister, this time Xavier Bertrand, urged communities to pay special attention to the old and vulnerable and to those living on their own. Medical students and retired doctors were brought in to help out in hospitals. To add to the problem, surgeons, anaesthetists and obstetricians had gone on strike at French private clinics in a row over fees and rising insurance premiums. French officials expressed fears that public hospitals would be overwhelmed during the heatwave, if private facilities were unavailable.

Similarly, across Europe and not least the UK, the 2006 heatwave was damaging crops. According to the London *Observer*, wheat crops in the UK, as a result of a scorching July, were down by a million tonnes, at least a 5 percent loss in production compared with recent years. In Poland, Agriculture Minister Andrzej Lepper, warned that the country's cereal harvest would slump by 20 percent because of the drought. Meanwhile, Dutch agriculture officials similarly warned that the country's potato crop was likely to be poor. Once again, the operation of nuclear power plants was affected and Spain's oldest nuclear power station — the Santa María de Garona plant — had to be shut down because of an excessive temperature rise in the waters of the Ebro river.

In their 1999 study, *Heatwaves in a Changing Climate,* Megan Gawith, Thomas Downing and Theodore Karacostas, look at the likelihood of increased heatwaves from global warming for two locations, Oxford in England and Thessaloniki in Greece. On the basis of the UK Met Office's climate models of the time, they come up with the disturbing prediction that southern England will suffer ten times more heatwaves than at present. Greece will suffer not only twice as many heatwaves, but whereas fifty hour events are relatively rare, they will become 100 hour events in the near future. Such heatwaves, combined with drought conditions will play havoc with most crops, and give rise to a high risk of bushfires or forest fires, such as Spain, Portugal and Greece have experienced recently. A worrying factor is that more recent climate models show global warming taking place far more rapidly and more intensely than previous predictions.

Such warnings seem to have been borne out by 2006's hot summer, when the United States was to experience similar extreme heat conditions. By the end of July, some 150 people had died in the western States as a result of the heat, most of the victims in California, including a man who died in a hospital emergency room after his body temperature had reached more than 43°C.

Millions or people suffering electricity blackouts were other consequences of the heatwave in California, the state electricity grid coming close to meltdown as reserves dropped below 5 percent. Air conditioners working at full blast, plus power-hungry plasma TVs contributed to the crisis. Between 1999 and 2003, the United States averaged nearly 900 heat-related deaths each year;

2006, with 132 deaths reported in central California alone, could well top that. California Dairies claimed that 16,500 cows or one percent of the state's dairy herd died during the heatwave, with the result that milk production fell by twenty percent. Under normal circumstances California provides some twelve percent of all milk within the United States.

July 2006's heatwave was still not as terrible as the scorching heat of the 1930s Dust Bowl years in the Mid West, but computer models suggest that heatwaves in the near future will leave the Dust Bowl years way behind. Warmer nights and drier days are the stuff of heatwaves and, according to a recent study published in the *Journal of Geophysical Research,* summer nights have been getting warmer over the past twenty-five years with less relief from the heat of the day. And, again in 2006, the Climate Research Unit in East Anglia, England, came to the conclusion that European summer heatwaves have increased in frequency at most stations since 1880 and will continue to do so as a result of human-induced global warming.

*The soil of the Rhine banks cracked from heat and aridity in Düsseldorf, Germany, in June 2005*
*[Martin Gerten, PAP]*

At a meeting in the Hague in November 2000, to thrash out the rules for the Kyoto Protocol, the secretary general, Professor Godwin Obasi, of the World Meteorological Organization, proclaimed that 'heatwaves are expected to become a major killer.' He referred in particular to the way in which small increases in global temperature from greenhouse gas emissions are amplified in cities. In the fifteen largest US cities, 'an average of 1,500 people collapse and die from heatwaves each year, a significant increase over the past decade. The annual death toll from heatwaves in those same cities is likely to reach 3,000 to 4,000 by 2020, a doubling of the raised numbers of 2000.'

The year 2005 did its best to confirm Obasi's fears. More than 200 cities in the United States broke all-time heat records and Reno in Nevada, set a new record with ten consecutive days above 38°C (100°F) with Tucson, Arizona, even surpassing that with its all-time record of thirty-nine consecutive days exceeding such temperatures. New Orleans, as well as the surrounding waters of the Gulf, also hit an all-time temperature high, quite aside from the terrible damage inflicted by Hurricane Katrina.

*The same city, Düsseldorf, flooded in January 2003 as the Rhine river burst its banks  [Martin Gerten, PAP]*

Heatwaves go with forest fires and withered crops. In September 2005, southern Spain and Portugal suffered drought, with half the normal rainfall, and that, combined with forest fires, unleashed copious quantities of carbon dioxide into the atmosphere. And, for the first time in living memory, African locusts invaded French fields. As a result of that summer, and the particularly dry months of July and August, 2003, Western Europe added to its greenhouse emissions from traffic and industry by some 500 million tonnes of carbon, all from forests and fields, as crops shrivelled, soils desiccated and trees burnt.

The year 1976 is synonymous with drought in the UK. In 1991, the UK Department of the Environment (now called DEFRA — Department of the Environment, Food and Rural Affairs) estimated that, were greenhouse gas emissions to rise at business-as-usual levels, the probability of a summer as hot as 1976 would increase a hundredfold, from 0.1 percent to 10 percent by 2030 and to 33 percent by 2050, hence once every three years. Again such predictions are based on older, more conservative climate models.

Let alone the evidence that global warming is proceeding apace, such an incidence would change the face of farming. And, by allowing ourselves the luxury of abandoning any pretext of self-sufficiency in food in the UK, we would have made ourselves dependent on imports to an even greater extent than today. All well and good, if the rest of the world is managing to produce more food than now, to feed a bigger own population, plus have surpluses to spare. But what if devastating droughts and floods destroy life-saving crops because of global warming?

If the UK were serious about the impacts of climate change and global warming, it would be doing everything in its power to maintain locally a productive and sustainable agriculture. Instead, because of globalization and liberal trade, we have become prey to market forces, allowing many of our farmers to go to the wall. Meanwhile, farm production has become ever more inefficient when we take stock of the inputs and well as outputs. Add in the air miles for transporting food across the planet, as much as 4,000 kilometres averaged out for items in the supermarket, and modern intensive agriculture becomes a significant drain on resources.

*OPPOSITE:*
*[Dain Hubley]*

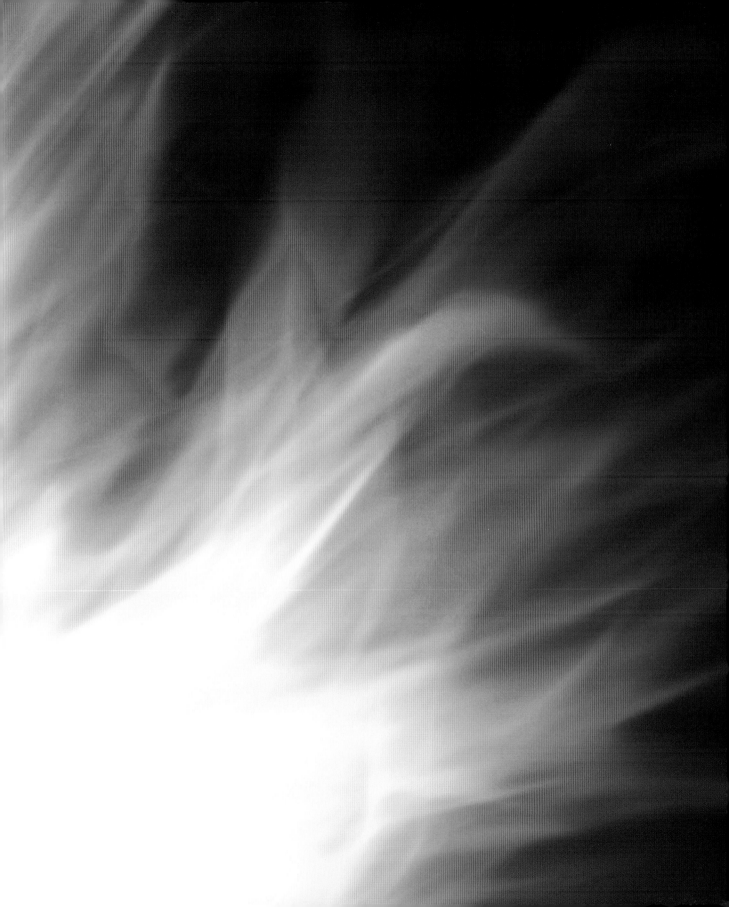

## The problem of water supplies

Heat waves and drought tend to go together, especially if rainfall patterns have changed significantly, leaving reservoirs low. Groundwater replenishment may prove to be an even greater problem, not only because of human needs but also because reduced groundwater can lead to surface instabilities and sinking. Climate change is having and will have an impact on water reserves, but according to a 2006 World Wildlife Fund report (WWF) poor management and the reliance, particularly in developed countries such as the UK, on nineteenth century piping, has just as important implications in terms of water provision as does climate change.

A number of cities in developed countries, London, Houston and Sidney, for example, are now using far more water than is being replenished and, according to the WWF, London is losing three hundred Olympic size swimming pools' worth of water every day because of ageing water mains. And, without the rains, agriculture will suffer fatally. Ian Curtis of the Oxfordshire Climate Change Project, envisages as many as thirty to forty days a year in Britain, in the near future, when temperatures will exceed 25°C, with all the attendant impact on water supplies. A warmer climate adds to water needs just at the very time when they are dwindling.

Southern Europe is also showing signs of water stress, because of a changing climate and add to that the shrinking of glaciers, which have until now played an important role in regulating the flow of freshwater, are dwindling fast. Once the glaciers have gone, then rainwater will run-off quickly into rivers and into the sea. And the cost of restraining the flow of water in rivers is extremely high, quite aside from the dangers of dams giving way and flooding downstream.

The Intergovernmental Panel on Climate Change (IPCC) predicts that within fifty years more than forty percent of the human population will suffer water shortages, as measured by clean drinking water. That will have a drastic impact on human health, quite aside from increasing many times the flood of environmental refugees.

Currently, as summed up in the IPCC's Third Assessment Report, 1.3 billion people do not have access to adequate supplies of safe water, and two billion people do not have access to adequate sanitation. Today, some nineteen countries, primarily in the Middle East and Africa, are classified as water-scarce or water-stressed.

*OPPOSITE:*
*[Luc Sesselle]*

Even in the absence of climate change, this number is expected to double by 2025, in large part because of increases in demand from population and economic growth. 'Climate change could further exacerbate the frequency and magnitude of droughts in some places, in particular central Asia, northern and southern Africa, the Middle East, the Mediterranean and Australia where droughts are already a recurrent feature.'

## Global warming and greenhouse gases

Working for CarboEurope, an European Union research team based in Jena, Germany, Philippe Ciais of the laboratory for Climate and Environmental Sciences in Paris, gathered data on soil and ecosystem emissions from one hundred sites across western Europe. His findings coincided with high emissions in the rest of the world: in

fact, 2003, with three parts per million of carbon dioxide emitted was an all-time record, even when compared with the previous record-breaking 2002.

2003 was also a bad year for the United States where, in the Midwest, corn crops failed and cattle died from heat stress. In New York City, the use of air conditioners led to a record demand for electricity. As in Europe during the dry years, Alon Angert and colleagues, at the University of California, Berkeley, found (*Proceedings of the National Academy of Sciences*, Vol. 102, p.10823) that, since the early 1990s, hot dry summers reduced the absorption of carbon dioxide by plants during their normal growing season. Meanwhile, Inez Fung, an atmospheric chemist at Berkeley, is unequivocal in her remarks that: 'Excess heating drives the dieback of forest, accelerates soil carbon loss and transforms the land from a sink to a source of carbon. Hotter temperatures amplify human-induced climate change.'

*In most areas in Australia, rainfall depends on El Niño which means that it is unpredictable from year to year and even more from decade to decade. Many European settlers had the bad luck to arrive during a lush period which led them to misjudge the climate and plant crops where they were not sustainable. In Australia, global warming is breaking down the pattern of reliable winter rains, causing great damage to agriculture. (Jared Diamond,* Collapse, *2006)*

We are learning about the impact of global warming all the time. Two years before the 2003 drought, CarboEurope estimated that Europe's ecosystems were absorbing between 7 and 12 percent of the continent's human induced carbon emissions. But, whereas CarboEurope might once have been right, it is becoming apparent that the situation has changed dramatically in the space of a year. CarboEurope scientists are now concerned that 2005, as well as 2006, will be bad years for emissions of carbon dioxide. That rather dashes the hopes of those who have argued that the fertilization effect of more carbon dioxide in the atmosphere, would compensate to a large extent the emissions from human activities.

*Effects of a long dry summer near Omeo, Victoria, Australia, in May 2005. The river has dried out and the pine trees boast the only green that is left.*  [Peter Firus]

Considerable quantities of carbon are stored in soils as organic matter left over from the growth of plants in previous years, even dating back thousands of years. What will global warming do to that carbon? Will it remain fixed in the soils and biomass? Again we have been taken by surprise; Guy Kirk, of Cranfield University in the UK, has been measuring changes in English and Welsh soils across the country since 1978. By returning each year to six thousand fixed points, Kirk and his colleagues were able to determine what was happening to living and decaying matter locked in pastures, croplands, forests, bogs, scrubland and heath. To their astonishment they found that carbon was being lost to the atmosphere at an average rate of 0.6 percent a year. The largest loss was from the richer soils, and when their findings were extrapolated to include the whole of Britain, the loss in carbon amounted to 13 million tonnes.

In the overall equation of carbon losses, we must take into account that the workings of agriculture are in themselves responsible for emissions and the richer the soils the more likely that they will be ploughed up on a regular basis, to grow annual crops. Nevertheless, global warming is having its impact, and soils are becoming responsible for a greater proportion of non-fossil carbon in the atmosphere than predicted. If that loss continues, says Kirk, 'the consequences of global warming will occur more rapidly. That's the scary thing. The amount of time we have got to do something about it is smaller than we thought.'

Averaged across the planet, the warmest ten years since records began in earnest in the early eighteenth century, have all occurred since 1990. That fact alone has been compelling evidence for a change in climate and that the culprit, so to speak, has been the emission of greenhouse gases. Virtually one year to the next has broken some record or another. In 1990, the hot, dry summer left 3,000 kilometres of rivers in France nearly empty and triggered widespread fires in the southern part of the country, as well as in Italy, Spain and Portugal.

1991 might well have followed suit, if it hadn't been for the eruption of Mount Pinatubo in the Philippines, which pumped aerosols high into the air. The aerosols reflected sunlight back into space and reduced temperatures at the Earth's surface by an average 1°C. As we clean up our act and prevent pollutants from getting into the atmosphere, for instance, by scrubbing dust and sulphur-containing compounds out of smoke-stacks, we could find ourselves facing a sudden rise in temperature; the obverse of what happened following Pinatubo's eruption.

## Mount Pinatubo, 1991

*ABOVE:*
*View across pyroclastic-flow deposits and fumarole in Marella River valley towards Pinatubo. The vegetation in the foreground is stripped and charred by ash-cloud surges of pyroclastic flows.* *[Willie Scott, USGS]*

*RIGHT:*
*Children on roof of school in Bamban, Tarlac. Their schoolhouse was buried by lahars (volcanic mudslides) of tributaries of the Bamban River.* *[Chris Newhall, USGS]*

'91 6 24

ABOVE:
*Aerial view of part of Clark Air Base showing buildings and vegetation damaged by tephra (ash) fall*
*[Willie Scott, USGS]*

LEFT:
*The June 29, 1991 eruption column from Mount Pinatubo*
*[Ed Wolfe, USGS]*

*Tree roots captured on a small river*
*in Salinas, Brazil  [Cesar Barreto]*

*BELOW LEFT:*
*Small clearings in a landscape of rainfor-*
*est will enhance convection and therefore*
*increase the rainfall*

*BELOW RIGHT:*
*Large clearings in rainforest lead to*
*reduced rainfall and so to die-back of the*
*remaining forest*

## Bringing drought to the rainforest

To speak of drought in the rainforest zones seems almost a contradiction in terms. To date climatologists have assumed that the amount of rainfall is dependent on the amount of forest and that as more and more of the forest is cut down and cleared, so rainfall will decline proportionately, akin to a straight line on a graph, until all the forest has gone. But by using a higher resolution 'mesoscale' modelling — therefore focussing on a limited region, in this instance Rondônia in Brazil's western Amazonia — Roni Avissar from Duke University in North Carolina, and Pedro Silva Dias from São Paulo, have uncovered a very different picture. Their studies show that rainfall actually increases when clearings are not too big, but then as the size of clearings increases, after a critical point the rainfall dwindles away rapidly and causes the remaining forest to crash.

When a clearing is no more than a certain size, probably no more than a few kilometres across, and if the forest around is relatively intact, then the mass of warm air that rises over the clearing, will suck in

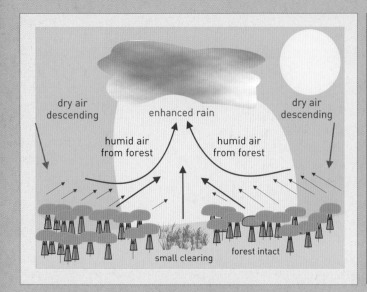

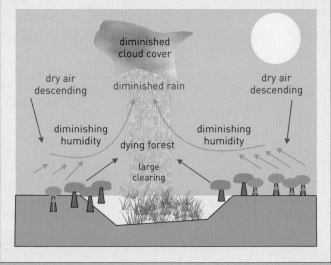

cooler, more humid, air from the surrounding forest. That convection process leads to the formation of thunderstorms. Under those circumstances rainfall will increase, perhaps by as much as 10 percent. On the other hand, make the clearing relatively large, when the forest is no longer large enough to moisten the up-draught of air, and the convection process literally runs out of steam. Rainfall then declines sharply.

One added effect of drying out is to make the forest increasingly vulnerable to fire, especially during dry years, such as are associated with strong El Niño events, like that of 1998, when vast areas of the state of Roraima in the northeast were ablaze.

*A person standing on parched earth at Dominguinhos, near the Amazon River in Brazil, October 2005. Members of the Brazilian government claimed that the warming of the Atlantic Ocean waters which unleashed a series of hurricanes in the Caribbean could be the cause of an intense drought that affected around 167,000 people in Brazilian Amazonia. [PAP]*

Dust storm over the Aral Sea  [NASA]

*Orphaned ship in former
Aral Sea, near Aral,
Kazakhstan, in 2003
[Staecker]*

## Aral Sea and 'man-made' droughts

The Aral Sea, an inland salt-water sea situated in Central Asia
between Kazakhstan and Uzbekistan, used to support a thriving
harbour and fishing industry on which many communities lived
happily. The salt levels of the lake were maintained in balance
by two freshwater rivers which fed into it. Up until the 1960s
it was the fourth largest inland water in the world. Now it has
shrunk to a third of its former size, and is surrounded by ship
cemeteries miles from the water's edge (see above). How did
this happen? It is a man-made disaster caused by the former
Soviet Union's decision to draw off water from the inflowing
rivers for irrigation purposes, so as to create vast areas of cotton
and rice plantations where once nothing grew. This has brought
prosperity to a new farming population while at the same time
drying out the Aral, with severe consequences in the surrounding region. Salt levels have risen to the surface and made water
tables too saline for human health, apart from the toxic effects of
pesticides and fertilizers used in the plantations, which are blown
in dust storms across the plains. As a result, local communities
suffer high levels of cancers and lung disease, with infant mortality much higher than before. Rusting ships are a reminder of a
way of life now gone, with no hope of ever being recovered.

## Drought and the Amazonian rainforest

Over the Amazon Basin, 2005 was a year without precedent. Never before in recorded history had the region, especially in Brazil, suffered such an extensive and devastating drought, not even in the years of strong El Niño events, when the Tropical Pacific Currents switch direction, and the trade winds, skimming over the surface from Africa to South America, falter and die away. 2005 should have been a normal, non-El Niño year, with strong trade winds picking up enormous volumes of water vapour from a warm tropical ocean, and dumping their load over the humid tropical Amazonian forests of Brazil.

But that is not what happened. Instead, the weather systems of the North Atlantic had transformed dramatically, with the Azores, normally a region of high pressure and sinking air, becoming a region of low pressure, with warm, moist air convecting upwards. Such a turn-around could explain in part why south-west Spain had its first ever tropical storm; why the hurricane track hit further south than normal, striking well within the Gulf of Mexico and washing out New Orleans into the bargain; it could also explain why the Caribbean coast of Colombia was subjected to unprecedented rains in November, causing widespread flooding and deaths; and why the central and western Amazon Basin was left high and dry.

During the Amazonian drought, river levels fell to their lowest ever, and Brazilian authorities declared four municipalities 'disaster areas' and another fourteen in a 'state of alert.' Fish died in their millions for lack of oxygen in the turgid waters of the myriad of tributaries that feed into the Amazon River, let alone in parts of the river itself.

A heavy layer of cold, dry air had formed close to the ground, encompassing hundreds of thousands of square kilometres, reaching right up into the Colombian Putumayo, and effectively preventing the convection process that leads to thunderstorms and rain. Held down by that layer, the smoke from the satellite count of 73,000 forest-clearance and spontaneous fires in Brazil had nowhere to go, except to make life extremely uncomfortable for people in Brazil, Peru and Colombia, who had to put up with a burning throat and smarting eyes for days on end. Aircraft were unable to land in Leticia and Tabatinga, the latter just across the border from Colombia and, when the smog was at its thickest, no-one dared make the crossing to the other side of the Amazon River for fear of colliding with a floating log, or worse still another boat.

What is deeply worrying is that 2006 threatened to be as bad, if not worse, than 2005. As the Brazilian ecologist Otavio Luz Castello remarked in July 2006, the waters of the Amazon were already draining away even faster than during 2005, 'and there are still more than three months of the dry season to go.' In the Jau National Park, eighteen hours upriver from Manaus, local people found it impossible to get to places they had previously reached without trouble, and the Brazilian State of Acre was without rain for an unprecedented forty days, and not surprisingly sandbanks were already beginning to surface in its rivers, in places allowing people to walk across the world's largest river channel.

Is global warming to blame? Certainly sea surface temperatures across the Caribbean have recently reached their highest ever recorded levels, not just spawning more hurricanes than ever before, but leaving coral reefs bleached of algae and dying (see p.44).

*Raimundo Landislay Pereira de Souza trying to make his way through dead fish on Rey Lake Vareza municipality in Brazil, October 2005. Around 100 tonnes of fish are believed to have died due to lack of oxygen in the area of the Brazilian Amazon.*
*[Raimundo Valentin, PAP]*

*Aerial view of the Igarape do Tupe, located some 20 kilometres from Manaus,
which shows signs of the severe drought that is affecting the lakes and rivers
of the Amazon Basin  [Raimundo Valentim, PAP]*

The loss of the reefs, the loss of mangrove swamps, all led to the coastline becoming ever more vulnerable to sea-level rise and storm surges. But, what about deforestation across the Latin American tropics and in particular across the Amazon Basin? Could deforestation, with resulting alterations in the transport out of the tropics of latent heat in the form of water vapour, have played a role? The answer is we do not know, not precisely that is, but, as we are being made increasingly aware, even small changes in heat transfer from the equator to the high latitudes, can have a profound effect on weather systems (see Chapter 5). What should worry us is whether the changes that occurred in 2005 across the tropical Atlantic could become a permanent feature. Were that to be the case, then we could see the demise of the great tropical rainforests that currently cover vast expanses of the Amazon Basin. Under those conditions, South America's agriculture may well not survive in its current form. And where would Brazil get its water to feed its hydroelectric dams that now supply some 80 percent of the country's electricity?

Dan Nepstad of the Woods Hole Oceanographic Institute concludes from his recent research in Santarém, Amazonia, that the rainforest cannot withstand more than two consecutive years of drought without breaking down. In year three, he says, the trees start dying. Beginning with the tallest they start crashing down, exposing the forest floor to the drying sun. Meanwhile, by the end of the year, the trees release more than two-thirds of the carbon dioxide they have stored during their lives. Nepstad concludes, 'Mega-fires are likely to sweep across the drying jungle. With the trees gone, the soil will bake in the sun and the rainforest could become desert.'

Already, from Tocantins right up to Guyana, we are seeing the Amazon Basin drying out and forming savanna, with its mixture of drought tolerant shrubs and grasses. That may well be the beginnings of desertification, indicating that the natural watering system over South America is breaking down; that the forests are no longer able to sustain themselves. And without the forests, all the countries in South America would suffer dramatic changes to their climate and rainfall. In essence it would be catastrophic. Nor would the rest of the planet escape.

# 3. Global Meltdown

## *The melting of the tundra*

You have spent your life feeling the ground firm under your feet and you are confident that's the way it is always going to be. Then, suddenly, that very same ground turns to mush, your house begins to sink, cracking apart as it slides deep into the ground, until finally it vanishes, engulfed by the very land that had once held it firm and upright. Robert Iyatunguk, one of six hundred Inupiat Eskimos in the village of Shishmaref, has seen it happen, has seen the houses go, has seen trees topple as their roots lose purchase. He lives some twenty miles south of the Arctic Circle, on a spit of land jutting into the ocean on the west coast of Alaska; his concern is that the land they live on will simply vanish, slipping bit by bit into the Bering Sea.

As 'erosion coordinator' for the village, Robert Iyatunguk's task is to record the disintegration taking place. In 2004, Mark Lynas, author of *High Tide: News from a Warming World,* met up with Robert and saw the damage for himself. Robert insisted that storms were more frequent, the winds stronger and the water getting ever higher.

'If we get 12 to 14 foot high waves this place is going to get wiped out in a matter of hours. We're in panic mode because of how much ground we are losing. If our airstrip gets flooded out, there goes our evacuation by plane.'

Something of that already happened in 1997, he went on to say, when a ferocious storm struck the island, washing away fifty feet of land, and taking houses on cliff tops with it.

In Canada's Yukon, life is not just getting tough for the Inuits, whose villages are breaking up further to the North, the melting ice also has appalling consequences for polar bears which find themselves adrift and away from their usual hunting grounds. As a result, the bears are dying in their hundreds.

Some one hundred kilometres away from the Alaskan border, in Canada's Dawson City, Yukon, with its population of 1,500, the melting of the permafrost is having disastrous consequences, too. Already, global warming has left its mark: spruce beetle infestations because of the milder winters, a rash of forest fires because of the drier summers, and spring floods because of melting ice.

*OPPOSITE:*
*[Randall Hop]*

## A way of life under threat

*Inupiat Eskimo Johnny Weyiouanna walks on melting ice on top of the frozen Chukchi Sea, June 9, 2005, in Shishmaref, Alaska, USA. Traditionally, spring seal hunting around the village of Shishnmaref has been done on the ice, by dog sled or snow machine, but climate change has forced the Eskimos to use their hand made boats, normally reserved for the fall hunt when the sea is clear of ice. They must drag the boats over the thinning ice to open water, where they must navigate between floating ice in search of seals. Climate warming has caused the Chukchi Sea, which surrounds the island, not to freeze before the arrival of the autumn storms, as it has for centuries, so leaving the island unprotected. In the last ten years, hundreds of feet of shore as well as several houses have been lost to the storms. Poised to become the world's first global warming refugees, Shishmaref's Inupiat Eskimos are struggling for their survival. [Gilles Mingasson/Getty Images]*

The underlying structure of the town is solid ice, but the top five metres of the permafrost contain groundwater which goes through a successive cycle of freezing and thawing, so raising and lowering the surface. A failure to take that 'active layer' into account can lead to disaster, as occurred when constructing the town's hockey arena in 2000. The builders, ignorant of the special conditions, made the mistake of pouring concrete over the active permafrost layer, without realizing they had trapped warm air. When temperatures fell to −40°C the air below the concrete pad contracted which caused the pad to become unstable, crack and break apart. That fundamental error bankrupted Dawson City and left the local government in disarray.

'If the permafrost fails here,' said Norm Carlson, responsible for the town's public works, in an interview with the Canadian *Globe and Mail* (06/03/06), 'everything is going to snap. It just can't take that kind of movement. Roads would melt, the whole town would sink. We would lose all our infrastructure wherever there is ice in the ground. It would be soup.'

*Permafrost tilting building in Dawson City, Yukon*
*[Richard G. Baker, University of Iowa]*

*Bumpy ride in Fairbanks, Alaska, where bumps are caused by melting ice wedges in the permafrost. The wedges were caused by cracks which started when the ground was very cold over 10,000 years ago. When meltwater gets in the cracks in spring, the ice thaws and the crack widens. In winter, this becomes an ice wedge of almost 100 percent ice, while the surrounding soil is about 50 percent ice. When they melt the ground drops by different amounts.*
*[Peter Essick/Aurora/Getty Images]*

In February 2006, a large municipal water pipe in Dawson dropped 25 centimetres at one joint causing it to fracture. It cost USD 20,000 to repair and that is just a tiny fraction of the mounting cost of shoring up the town, which in 2005 alone amounted to USD 600,000. The public works budget for 2006 was already one million US dollars.

Ottawa's Carleton University has conducted a twenty-year long study of the effects of climate change on permafrost in the North, including central Yukon. One factor which has warmed the ground is the insulating effect of greater than average snowfalls which Dawson has experienced over the past three winters. Geography professor Dr Chris Burn has been based at Mayo, some 200 kilometres east of Dawson, since the 1980s when the study began, and carrying out measurements on local temperatures. He reports that, in the three years to 2006, the summer temperature of Mayo's soil jumped to 6.5 degrees from 5.5.

## Global warming and the polar regions

Global warming appears to be having its biggest impact in the polar extremities and both regions are vying with each other as to which is warming the most rapidly. In the Arctic, Gunter Weller, at the Center for Global Change and Arctic Systems Research in Fairbanks, Alaska, has seen average annual temperatures rise over the State by more than 3°C and as much as 4.5°C during the winter — a rate of warming, he told Mark Lynas, that is ten times greater than the rest of the world ('Meltdown,' *The Guardian,* February 14, 2004)

'We've seen great changes in temperature, but also in the physical environment,' Weller said. 'Glaciers are melting, permafrost thawing and the sea-ice is reduced. We've seen a slow encroachment of the boreal forests northwards — so tundra is slowly being overtaken by forests ... we see changes everywhere.' Not least of those changes has been to overland transportation. Less than half a century ago, a truck could drive across the Alaska tundra for an average 225 days. Now, the tundra will support heavy vehicles for only 75 days during the year.

According to David Lawrence of the National Center for Atmospheric Research in Boulder, Colorado, as much as 90 percent of the permafrost in Arctic soils could vanish over the coming decades. Until recently, one quarter of the land surface of the northern hemisphere remained frozen all year round, but that is changing as the atmosphere warms. By modelling the impact of global warming, Lawrence comes up with a worrying scenario of permafrost melting down three metres or more right across Canada, Alaska, Siberia and northern Scandinavia. Highways will buckle, buildings tumble, pipelines twist and break. The ecology of the region will be transformed, especially as the treeline advances ever northwards. It's a positive feedback situation, because the firs, with their dark evergreen needles and their ability to shed snow, will warm up in the first rays of the spring sunshine, causing more snow to melt and exposing the permafrost to more heating. It doesn't look as if the thawing is going to stop; on the contrary, it's set to get worse.

*NEXT PAGE:*
*'Drunken forest' of spruce trees where there has been permafrost melt. The trees no longer find support in the softened ground. North of Fairbanks, Alaska.*
*[Peter Essick/Aurora/Getty Images]*

*Ilulissat is a town in Greenland on the Ilulissat ice fjord. Ilulissat's fjord and glacier, a UNESCO heritage site, are major contributors to the mass balance of the continental ice-sheet. The glacier has shrunk by over 10 kilometres over the last few years, as an alarming consequence of global warming.* [Peter Bartlett]

## What the Greenland ice-sheet tells us

The Greenland ice-sheet — two miles thick and broad enough to blanket an area the size of Mexico — shapes the world's weather, matched in influence only by Antarctica in the Southern Hemisphere. From cores of ancient Greenland ice extracted by the National Science Foundation, researchers have identified at least twenty sudden climate changes in the last 110,000 years, in which average temperatures fluctuated as much as 15 degrees in a single decade.

Should all of the ice-sheet ever thaw, the melt-water could raise sea-level 23 feet and swamp the world's coastal cities, home to a billion people. It would cause higher tides, generate more powerful

*Aerial view of drifting ice in Ofjordes Greenland  [Hinrich Baesemann, PAP]*

storm surges and, by altering ocean currents disrupt the global climate. Weather patterns in northern Europe would be drastically affected.

All the evidence shows that, the glaciers of Greenland are melting twice as fast as they were five years ago, even as the ice-sheets of Antarctica — the world's largest reservoir of fresh water — are also shrinking. There is no escaping the worldwide consequences of such a rapid change, and the most recent climate projections have now had to take this into account.

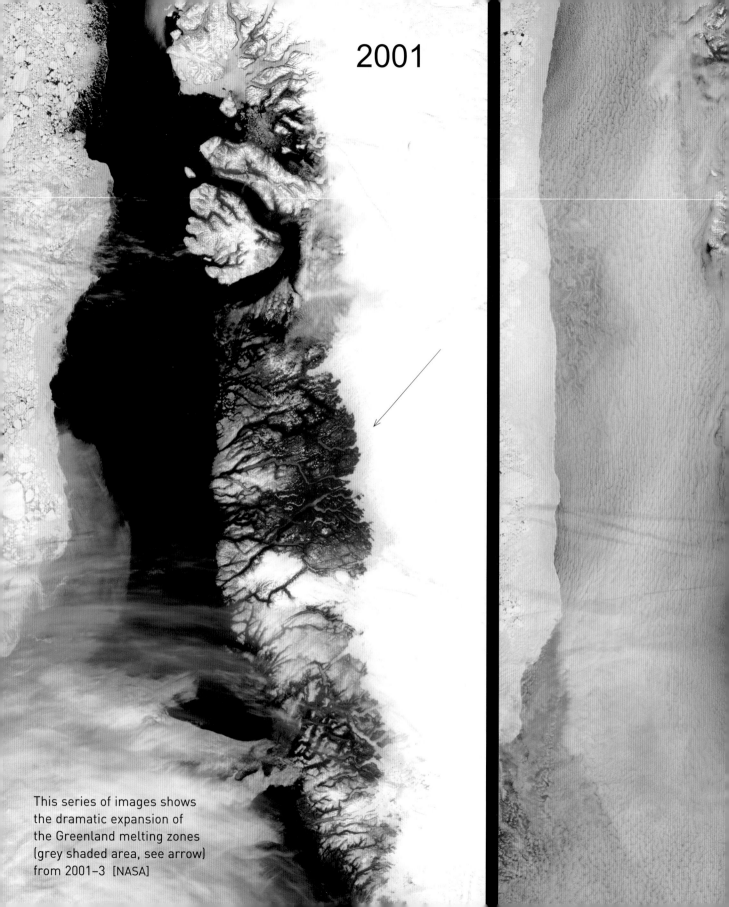

2001

This series of images shows
the dramatic expansion of
the Greenland melting zones
(grey shaded area, see arrow)
from 2001–3  [NASA]

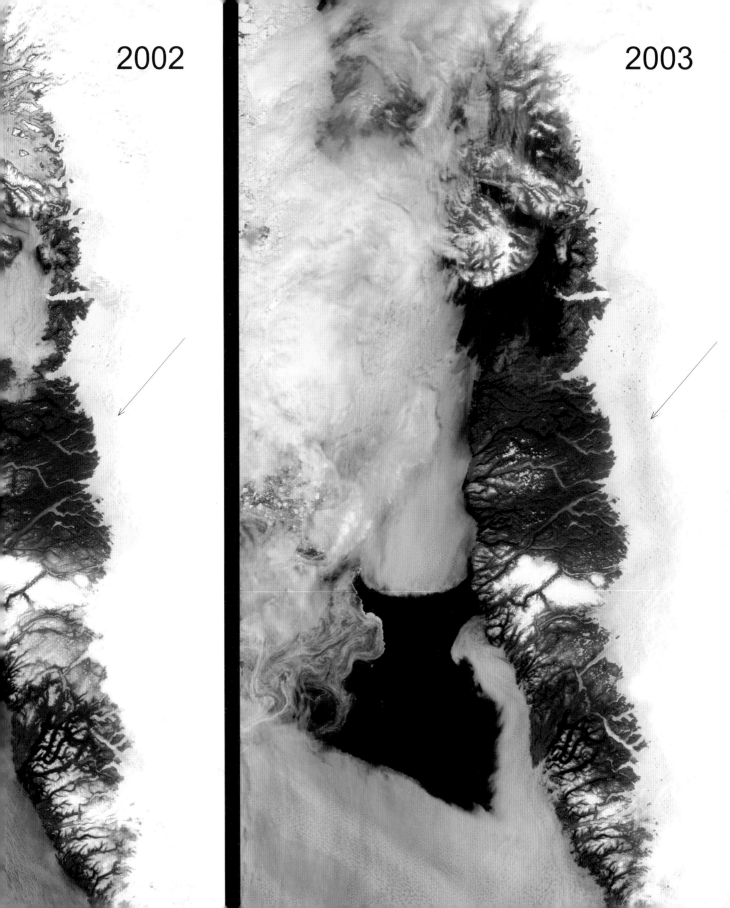

2002

2003

*How Greenland is turning green*

Lichens, grass and flowers are growing again in areas of Greenland where there has been only ice for millions of years. And farmers are returning to work land which has been locked in ice for centuries, since the time of the Vikings. What has happened over the last 150 years is a huge retreat of Greenland's glaciers as they melt and leave the soil and rock exposed, in most recent years at the alarming rate of disappearance of 10 metres per year. Satellite images already show record levels of melting in 2002 and 2004, leaving the ice-cap full of pools of blue water, which can then penetrate below the ice and start a process of slippage making the ice unstable.

As the ice melts, freshwater flows off the vast ice-cap and joins the North Atlantic, while icebergs break away and float off into the ocean, now at an unparalleled rate. One of the best places to see them is Ilulissat, meaning 'the town of icebergs,' the third largest town in Greenland. It is 250 km north of the polar circle in Disko Bay at the mouth of a 45 km long fjord which since July 2004 is on the UNESCO World Heritage List. Huge icebergs, calved by the nearby Sermeq Kujalleq glacier, float along the fjord to the sea, some 100 metres high, at a rate of more than twenty million tons of ice a day. Residents there say the pattern is now changing, with the icebergs smaller and more numerous than before.

The potential for a devastating change in global sea-levels is starting to concern scientists. For the ice-sheets represented by Greenland together with Antarctica, covering some ten percent of the world's land surface, are on average 2,500 metres thick and hold some 77 percent of the Earth's freshwater. If the Greenland ice-sheet were to melt, sea-levels could rise by 23 feet (7 metres), according to estimates from the U.N.-affiliated Intergovernmental Panel on Climate Change. Recent reports of observations of the entire ice-sheet from NASA's Grace Earth observation satellite (December 2005) show that the volume of Greenland's ice is shrinking by 162 cubic kilometres (39 cubic miles) per year, higher than all previously published estimates. The resulting ice-melt is already contributing 0.4 millimetres (.016 inches) per year to global sea-level rise.

Iceberg counts are also affected by the rapid break-up of the massive ice-sheet. International Ice Patrol records, which go back more than 120 years, show their seasonal severity index (based on icebergs which cross the 48°N latitude) reached three peaks in the last twenty years or so. The pattern there, too, may well be changing.

*The threat of carbon emissions*

Mounds of sedge moss in the tundra and permafrost regions of the Arctic Circle grow on their ancestors, gradually raising the surface, such that the top living layer may be many feet higher than the base. That millennial growth leads to the accumulation of enormous quantities of carbon. As a result, the permafrost regions probably contain as much stored carbon as the total found in the atmosphere. If the carbon were to be released with the melting of the permafrost, that would cause major global warming.

Such releases, worrying in the extreme, are now taking place across the tundra but especially in Siberia. Katey Walter of the University of Alaska, Fairbanks, told a meeting of the Arctic Research Consortium in May 2005 that methane, bubbling out from thawing permafrost, was preventing freezing even in the depths of the winter. In Siberia the peat bogs remain wet enough such that the carbon is released in the form of methane, which weight per weight, has a greenhouse impact twenty times that of carbon dioxide. On the other hand, if the peat bogs dry out, the methane gets oxidized to carbon dioxide before venting. In all, several hundred gigatonnes of carbon could be released, enough to send global temperatures soaring.

Having spent a good deal of his time digging down through sedge moss mounds in Alaska, Lee Klinger of the US National Center for Atmospheric Research, in Boulder, Colorado, has come to realize what an important role sphagnum moss may play in the Earth's energy budget. First, they form a major carbon sink by drawing carbon dioxide down out of the atmosphere. But that is by no means all. Despite the cold, the moss grows reasonably well in high latitude regions, especially when conditions are wet and marshy, and the soils acidic, as they tend to be when formed from marine sediments, with their high concentrations of sulphur compounds. Over much of the year temperatures are close to freezing and the whole area tends to be enshrouded for much of the time in mists and fogs. The bleak foggy atmosphere maintains the chill, its high albedo reflecting sunlight back into space.

Bacterial action in the soil turns the sulphur into sulphuric acid which is well tolerated by the moss while hindering the growth of conifers. Meanwhile, through its steady growth and decay over thousands of years the moss lays down layer upon layer of peat. That burial, by taking carbon out of the atmosphere leads over time to higher oxygen levels in the atmosphere. Under the dry conditions of an ice age, when the moss is spreading at the expense of

*NEXT PAGE:*
*Polar bear sitting on melting ice,*
*Franz Josef land, Artic sea*
*[Per Breiehagen]*

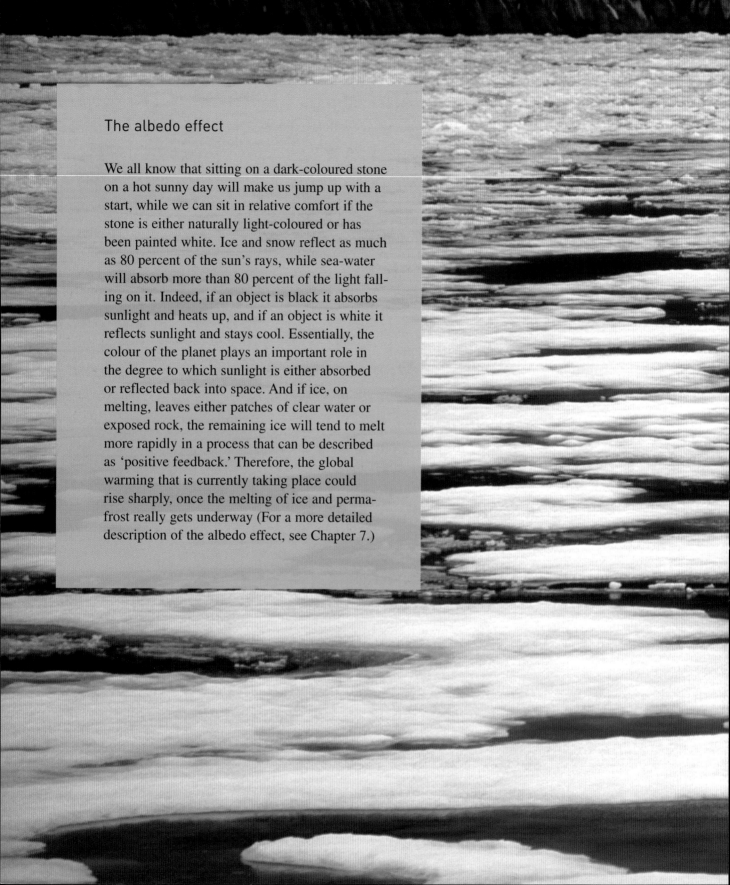

## The albedo effect

We all know that sitting on a dark-coloured stone on a hot sunny day will make us jump up with a start, while we can sit in relative comfort if the stone is either naturally light-coloured or has been painted white. Ice and snow reflect as much as 80 percent of the sun's rays, while sea-water will absorb more than 80 percent of the light falling on it. Indeed, if an object is black it absorbs sunlight and heats up, and if an object is white it reflects sunlight and stays cool. Essentially, the colour of the planet plays an important role in the degree to which sunlight is either absorbed or reflected back into space. And if ice, on melting, leaves either patches of clear water or exposed rock, the remaining ice will tend to melt more rapidly in a process that can be described as 'positive feedback.' Therefore, the global warming that is currently taking place could rise sharply, once the melting of ice and permafrost really gets underway (For a more detailed description of the albedo effect, see Chapter 7.)

boreal forests, the peat becomes vulnerable to fires that can burn unquenchably, consuming oxygen and releasing carbon dioxide and nitrogen oxides. Almost unquenchable peat bog fires have become commonplace in Kalimantan, as a result of clearing and burning the tropical rainforest to make way for African palm.

As the levels of carbon dioxide once again rise in the atmosphere so the planet warms up and gives the trees the opportunity they were waiting for. To complete the cycle, carbon dioxide is gradually taken out of the atmosphere, forming organic compounds that build up in the sediments, such as the methane hydrates that can be found overlying continental shelves, as off the Amazon coast of Brazil. Similarly, on the other side of the coin, oxygen levels gradually rise in the atmosphere, encouraging forest fires and peat fires to ignite more easily, which again start mopping up the oxygen and releasing carbon dioxide.

### Warming in Antarctica

Antarctica is also getting its fair share of warming. A British Antarctic Survey team from Cambridge, led by John Turner, has found that atmospheric temperatures in the middle troposphere over Antarctica have increased at a rate of 0.5 to 0.7°C per decade over the past thirty years. Once again, it can be little more than conjecture that the global warming is the result of anthropogenic emissions of greenhouse gases, but, given that climatic changes are coming thick and fast, it becomes ever more likely that human beings are implicated through greenhouse gas emissions from our industrial activities. Two consequences of the atmospheric warming are greater snowfall because of increased humidity and sea-level rise as the ice-sheets of west Antarctica become less stable and start melting (*New Scientist,* March 8, 2006, p.7).

In fact, huge ice-streams are now draining off from the Pacific sector of the West Antarctic ice-sheet, therefore adding to the load of freshwater from collapsing ice-shelves. In a decade the flow has increased tenfold or more and is resulting in a sea-level rise of an additional 0.18 millimetres per year. The loss of the West Antarctic ice-sheet alone would cause the average sea-level to rise by as much as 2 metres. But when would that be? In its Third Assessment Report of 2001, the Intergovernmental Panel on Climate Change (IPCC) came to the conclusion that it would take several centuries of global warming to bring about the loss of the ice-sheet.

Once again, it appears that the consensus of scientists who participated in the United Nations Framework for Climate Change have underestimated the rate of change. In March 2002, 500,000 million million tonnes of ice slipped into the Weddell Sea, as the Larsen B ice-shelf of the Antarctic collapsed. The shelf was 200 metres thick and covered an area of 3,250 square kilometres. It took just thirty-one days for the whole process. Also in March of that year a tongue of ice covering an area of 5,500 square kilometres broke off from the Antarctic Continent and formed a massive iceberg called B22.

Just as takes place in the Arctic with regard to ocean currents, an excess of freshwater in the Antarctic could lead to critically important currents becoming suppressed. Upwellings, pushing from the depths and breaking through to the surface, bring essential nutrients for plankton, and plankton, as the bottom of the food chain, are essential for the rest of marine life. Phytoplankton also serve another purpose in helping to generate marine stratus clouds that help cool the ocean surface by reflecting sunlight.

The Humboldt Current, which flows northwards from Antarctica, and then wells-up along the Peruvian coast of South America, gives us a vivid reminder of the importance of such currents in sustaining the marine ecosystem. As it happens, the Humboldt Current is suppressed during El Niño years, when the surface waters of the tropical Pacific Ocean switch from flowing to the east and reverse direction to one in which the warm surface waters pile up against the South American coastline, rather like water slopping from one side of a bath to another. El Niño events occur every few years, generally last for a year, and rebound to La Niña events when the Pacific Ocean settles for several years at a time in a regime of east-to-west flow of the surface waters.

## The effect of ice-melt on oceans

One consequence of the polar thawing is that run-off of freshwater into the ocean has been increasing in recent years, and this in turn affects weather around the world. Rainfall has also increased, presumably because of the warmer atmosphere and ocean. A net result is that enormous areas in western Siberia are now melting, according to Sergei Kirpotin, a botanist at Tomsk State University who has been investigating the region with Judith Marquand of

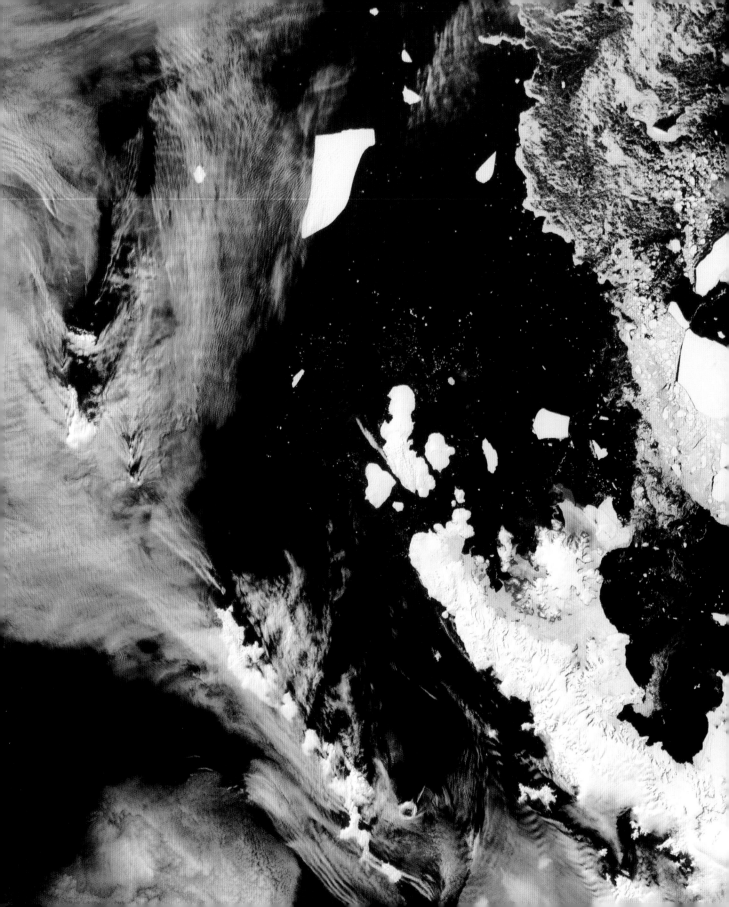

Antarctic Peninsula and
Weddell Sea, 2001  [NASA]

Oxford University. They find that a permafrost area of one million square kilometres is transforming into thousands of shallow lakes. Kirpotin talks of an 'ecological landslide that is probably irreversible and is undoubtedly connected to global warming.' The entire sub-Arctic region is melting. 'This has all happened in the last three to four years.' (Fred Pearce, *New Scientist,* August 11, 2005)

Besides making life pretty uncomfortable for those living in regions of tundra, the melting is having major climatic consequences, primarily by adding a load of freshwater to the surface waters in the Arctic Circle. In fact, Siberian rivers, such as the Ob, which disgorge into the Arctic ocean, are now flowing at double the rate of a decade back. Melting sea-ice is adding to the load of freshwater and the dilution of the Arctic Ocean.

Dr James Hansen, from NASA's Goddard Institute in New York, has been reviewing satellite images which show that the Greenland ice-cap is disintegrating much more rapidly than anticipated in the models of climatologists, including those who contributed to the IPCC's Third Assessment Report of 2001. 'Twice as much ice is going into the sea, as it was five years ago,' he said in an interview with Fred Pearce. 'The implications for rising sea-levels — and climate change — could be dramatic.' *(The Independent,* February 17, 2006)

For the first time, because of satellite advances, Hansen reported, 'we are seeing the detailed behaviour of the ice-streams that are draining the Greenland ice-sheet. The images show that Greenland seems to be losing at least 200 cubic kilometres of ice a year. It is different from even two years ago, when people still said the ice-sheet was in balance.

'Hundreds of cubic kilometres sounds like a lot of ice. But this is just the beginning. Once a sheet starts to disintegrate, it can reach a tipping point beyond which break-up is explosively rapid. The issue is how close we are getting to that tipping point. The summer of 2005 broke all records for melting in Greenland. So we may be on the edge.'

Hansen made the point that we have only just come to understand for the first time how the melting process works in a vast ice-sheet, pointing out that the models traditionally used to investigate this are 'almost worthless.' Instead of the ice-sheet behaving like a single huge block of ice, what happens is much more dynamic, triggered by the melted ice-streams forming lakes which then penetrate below the surface and cause slippage towards the ocean.

'Our Nasa scientists have measured this in Greenland. And once these ice-streams start moving, their influence stretches right to the interior of the ice-sheet. Building an ice-sheet takes a long time, because it is limited by snowfall. But destroying it can be explosively rapid.

'How fast can this go? Right now, I think our best measure is what happened in the past. We know that, for instance, fourteen thousand years ago sea-levels rose by 20m in four hundred years — that is five metres in a century.'

Hansen believes that sea-level rise will be more of an issue than the global warming that brought it about. 'It's hard to say what the world will be like if this happens,' he says. 'It would

*Glacier Perito Moreno, Patagonia region, El Calafate, Argentina*
*[Robert Flaum]*

be another planet. You could imagine great armadas of icebergs breaking off Greenland and melting as they float south. And, of course, huge areas being flooded. How long have we got? We have to stabilize emissions of carbon dioxide within a decade, or temperatures will warm by more than one degree ... we don't have much time left.'

### The working of the Gulf Stream

The unlikely and surprising sight of palm trees in Devon and Cornwall, counties which make up the extreme south-west region of Britain, and in gardens on the west coast of Scotland, is due to a warm Atlantic ocean current known as the Gulf Stream. The Gulf Stream depends on cold, dense, saline waters of the Arctic Circle and the northern reaches of the Atlantic Ocean, sinking and flowing back along the bottom of the ocean towards the tropics and then on to the Southern Ocean and even up into the Indian Ocean. To make up for the sinking water, warm surface waters flow from the tropics, helped on their way by prevailing south-westerly winds. The entire circulation system from the tropics and back takes a thousand years or more to complete.

Part of the process depends on the evaporation of water from the ocean during the summer months. That leaves saltier water behind which, on freezing in the winter months, gains sufficient density to sink — hence what is termed the thermohaline circulation. The degree of sinking could be changing as a result of two factors, first, warmer temperatures because of global warming and, second, the influx of freshwater from increased glacier melting in Greenland and from river discharge into the Arctic Circle. The dilution of the surface waters takes place even though a warmer atmosphere will evaporate more water from the oceans. The net result is to slow down the sinking of the surface waters, and, like a blocked motorway lane, the Gulf Stream stalls, so cutting off the northward flow of the warm waters of the tropics.

Just in the top hundred metres or so of the surface waters, the Gulf Stream has a flow equivalent to more than one hundred times the flow of all freshwater rivers and streams put together. In effect it carries more than one thousand terawatts of energy ($10^{15}$ watts), which is close to one hundred times the total primary energy used by human beings across the planet, and it warms the United Kingdom by as much as 8°C, especially during the winter months.

In fact, the North Atlantic offers a clear run to the Arctic Circle and the Gulf Stream can therefore carry its warm waters far to the north, in what is known as the North Atlantic Drift. Without that warm water current, northern Europe and Scandinavia would have a climate

*OPPOSITE:*
*A large section of ice falling off the Hubbard Glacier in Alaska*
*[Randall Hop]*

## What about Iceland?

Iceland has a complex micro-climate that touches on several core issues of the current climate debate. Originally about a quarter of Iceland was covered in woodland, most of which was quickly used up by the first settlers, or simply burnt to make room for pastures that were then overgrazed. Ever since Iceland has suffered severe erosion, exacerbated by yearly snowmelt and strong winds. The harsh northern climate slows or prevents the recovery of soil and vegetation. (Jared Diamond, *Collapse,* 2006)

Iceland is at the junction of cold and warm air and ocean currents. A 1°C change in annual temperature can alter hay production by 20 percent in the fertile regions. Changes in ocean circulation and temperature affect fish stock upon which the Icelanders heavily depend. Warmer temperatures increase meltwater flow and benefit hydro-power production but also increase the danger of flooding and land erosion. Sea level rise is another worry as most settlements are located along the coast. (http://www.scotland.gov.uk)

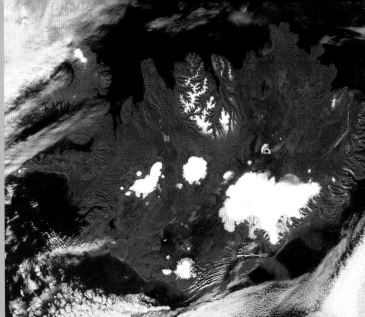

The harsh climate that might be expected based on Iceland's closeness to the Arctic Circle is softened by the tail end of the Gulf Stream current, which flows up through the Atlantic Ocean bringing heat from the tropics. Unlike its eastern neighbour Greenland, large portions of Iceland shake off their wintry cover each year. (http://earthobservatory.nasa.gov)

*BELOW:*
*An icebird with fledgling, iceberg on*
*Jökulsárlón, Iceland  [Andreas Tille]*

*Travelling northwards, the Gulf Stream divides into two streams, one that continues northwards and another that forms a sub-tropical gyre at just about the latitude of Portugal. This southern branch switches direction and runs back down the coast of Africa, then across the Atlantic Ocean towards South America. The northern branch of the Gulf Stream then itself divides into two, one stream passing to Greenland and the other round the coast of Britain and on to Scandinavia. Meanwhile, the water that sinks courses over the ocean bottom, drawing in more water from the surface behind it. The entire circulation system from the tropics and back takes a thousand years or more to complete.*

akin to Labrador in Canada. Instead, courtesy of the Gulf Stream and the warm winds and rain that come in with the westerlies, regions like Cornwall western Scotland and Scandinavia have a reasonably warm temperate climate that at times verges on the sub-tropical.

Certainly over the past century we have taken the Gulf Stream pretty well for granted, grateful for it making Britain such a green and pleasant land. But, scarily, that may be changing and much faster than climatologists had predicted. Harry Bryden and his group, at the Southampton Oceanography Centre in the UK, have been measuring the flow rate of the Gulf Stream by stringing a set of instruments across the Atlantic from the Canaries to the Bahamas. They come up with results that suggest that the flow of the northwards stream has fallen by as much as 30 percent compared with previous surveys carried out in 1957, 1981 and 1992. That finding appears to be corroborated by data collected in 1998, but not previously analysed by the United States National Oceanic and Atmospheric Administration.

Is the change for real, a consequence of global warming that has tipped some balance since 1992? Or could it just be part of natural variability, part of some cycle, a climatic oscillation involving the north Atlantic? Richard Wood, chief oceanographer at the UK Met Office's Hadley Centre for climate research in Exeter, is not wholly

## The stalling of the Gulf Stream?

Climate models of the thermohaline circulation suggest that the North Atlantic Drift would judder to a halt, at least in its northern branch, were the freshwater flow there to reach around 100,000 tonnes (cubic metres) per second. That translates into 3153.6 cubic kilometres per year, and therefore uncomfortably close to the average amount delivered to the entire Arctic Ocean over the course of the year from all freshwater run-off from the land, namely some 3,300 cubic kilometres. Currently, that input adds some 30 centimetres of freshwater to the surface of the Arctic Ocean each year, thereby substantially reducing its salinity and density, but not to the point of stopping the formation and sinking of heavy, cold, salty water.

   The degree of sinking could now be changing as a result of two factors: first, warmer temperatures because of global warming and, second, the influx of freshwater from increased glacier melting in Greenland and from river discharge into the Arctic Circle. The dilution of the surface waters takes place even though a warmer atmosphere will evaporate more water from the oceans. The net result is to slow down the sinking of the surface waters and, like a blocked motorway lane, the Gulf Stream stalls, so cutting off the northward flow of the warm waters of the tropics.

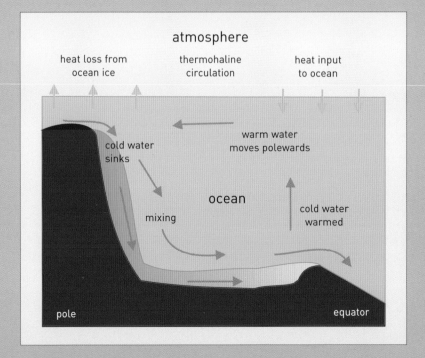

*Without the warm waters of the Gulf Stream flowing northwards, northern Europe and Scandinavia would experience winters as cold as Labrador*

convinced that the Gulf Stream is seizing up. The changes are so large, he says, they should have cut oceanic heating of Europe by about one-fifth — enough to cool the British Isles by 1°C and Scandinavia by 2°C. 'We haven't seen it yet,' he points out.

Others, such as Bryden's colleague Stuart Cunningham, believed that the findings are robust and that changes in the circulation are definitely taking place. The main change is in the European branch of the Gulf Stream where flow may have diminished by one half. Perhaps, the predicted fall in temperature as a result of a decline in the warm surface waters reaching up alongside northern Europe has been countered by a generalized rise in temperature brought on by the emissions of greenhouse gases?

Most climate models dealing with ocean circulation show that past a certain point, perhaps at the end of the century, global warming could cause the Gulf Stream to falter, but they haven't predicted it happening now. Serious side effects would be a shift in sea-levels, with as much as one metre of water piling up against the shoreline of northern Europe and an equivalent lowering in the Southern Ocean. Higher sea-levels on that scale would make coastlines much more vulnerable to storm surges, especially along the eastern seaboard of the United States (Stephen Battersby, *New Scientist,* pp.43–46, April 15, 2006).

Disturbingly too, Richard Wood finds from his models of the curtailment of the Gulf Stream that the monsoon rains over India would diminish significantly, reducing agricultural productivity by a third or more. Nor would the rainforests of the Amazon Basin be immune from such a change in the North Atlantic Conveyer circulation. As we shall see (Chapter 5), the integrity of the Amazon rainforests plays a critical role in the hydrological cycle, not just of South America, but of the entire planet. It is becoming evident that we cannot consider one part of the ocean-atmosphere circulation separate from the other. All are tightly integrated.

## Glaciers

Under 'normal' conditions, glaciers slide slowly, if not remorse-lessly, down mountain slopes. The sliding comes from the lubricating water that forms as the weight and pressure of the glacier bears down on the lower layers of ice. The physical action of melting is no different from that of a skater who can shift at breakneck speed, as well as whirl around, on an ice skating rink, but this time it is the skater's weight bearing down on the thin band of metal on the bottom side of the skate that does the trick of melting a strip of ice, which then freezes again as the skater moves on. If, in their sliding, glaciers slip into a warmer clime they will then melt all the more rapidly, altering the balance between the make-up of ice from snow that has fallen and that which is lost. Glaciers also lose bulk through a process known as 'ablation' in which ice transforms directly into water vapour in the atmosphere.

Glaciers are dangerous not just because of the crevasses and slipperiness; they can become monsters bearing death and destruction. As Robin McKie reported in *The Observer* (November 20, 2005), the Himalayas are becoming a threat to millions of people as a result of an unprecedented rate of melting. What happened in Ghat, Nepal, some twenty years ago, in 1985, is a dire warning. Lucky for Nawa Jigtar and his fellow villagers that they were up and about, giving them time to scramble to safety, when a terrible roaring sent them rushing out of their homes. A wall of water, hurtling down the slopes, simply swept the village away and, to Jigtar's horror, carried all his cattle with it. 'If it had been night,' said Jigtar, 'none of us would have survived.'

A survey of what happened showed that a lake, high in the Himalayas, burst its banks after its walls of rock and ice simply gave way because of glacier meltwaters. Several million cubic metres of water were unleashed to rampage down to the bottom of the valley.

*This panorama was shot while crossing a glacier on the northern side of Nanga Parbat (8125 m), Kashmir, the ninth highest peak on earth*
*[Waqas Usman, http://pbase.com/waqas]*

*This image shows the termini of the glaciers in the Bhutan-Himalaya. Glacial lakes have been rapidly forming on the surface of the débris-covered glaciers in this region during the last few decades. USGS researchers have found a strong correlation between increasing temperatures and glacial retreat in this region. According to Jeffrey Kargel, a USGS scientist, glaciers in the Himalaya are wasting at alarming and accelerating rates, as indicated by comparisons of satellite and historic data, and as shown by the widespread, rapid growth of lakes on the glacier surfaces. [NASA]*

Once rare, such incidents are becoming ever more common, with a tenfold increase just over the past two decades. Scientists pin the blame on global warming and warn that Himalayan glacier lakes are filling up, as more and more ice melts. In Bhutan, twenty-four glacial lakes are waiting to burst their banks, and a similar number in Nepal.

Nepal's Khumbu glacier, where Hillary and Tenzing began their 1953 Everest expedition has retreated three miles since their ascent. The head of the Nepal Mountaineering Association, Tashi Jangbu Sherpa, says, 'Hillary and Tenzing would now have to walk two hours to find the edge of the glacier which was close to their original base camp.' (Reuters, Environmental News Network, June 7, 2002). McKie reports that almost 95 percent of Himalayan glaciers are shrinking, which, because of increased winter flow and reduced summer flow, has profound implications for the entire region, therefore not just for Nepal and Bhutan, but for China, India and Pakistan.

Eventually, the Himalayan glaciers will shrink so much that rivers fed on the glacier melt, including the Indus, Yellow River and Mekong, will turn to mere trickles. Drinking and irrigation water will disappear. Hundreds of millions of people will be affected. As Dr Phil Porter, of the University of Hertfordshire points out, 'There

is a short-term danger of too much water coming out the Himalayas and a greater long-term danger of there not being enough.'

A report in *Nature* (November 2005) indicates that temperatures in the region have increased by more than 1°C recently and are set to rise by a further by at least 3°C within the century. 'A glacier lake catastrophe happened once in a decade fifty years ago,' said UK geologist John Reynolds. 'Five years ago, they were happening every three years. By 2010, a glacial lake catastrophe will happen every year.'

Nepal is now selling hydropower electricity to India and other countries, but those plants could be destroyed in the years to come. 'A similar lake burst near Machu Picchu in Peru,' says Reynolds, 'recently destroyed an entire hydro-electric plant. The same thing is waiting to happen in Nepal.'

In fact, the world's glaciers, with rare exception, have been shrinking to the point of vanishing altogether. The World Glacier Monitoring Service in Zurich, Switzerland, found that of eighty-eight glaciers surveyed in 2002 and 2003, just four were growing and seventy-nine or more were receding. Is global warming to blame? The answer is hard to tease out from what may be nothing more than natural variability: glaciers come and go over a cycle

*Peruvian residents of the Machu Picchu district of the Andean mountains cry as they view the damage to their homes, April 11, 2004, following a landslide which struck the region the day before*
*[Oscar Paredes, PAP]*

lasting thousands of years. But one thing is certain, once the ice has retreated, the rock beneath exposes a dark surface to the sun and consequently the absorption of solar energy and therefore heating of the immediate surroundings will cause any ice in the locality to melt faster in a process of positive feedback. The more the ice vanishes the faster the remainder will melt.

Mount Kilimanjaro is a good case in point, having lost most of its glaciers since measurements of more than a century ago. The Andean tropics have also begun losing glaciers and, over the past fifty years, they have lost more than half of their glaciers. The Meteorological Office of Colombia (IDEAM) has warned that, were global warming to continue, most of the country's remaining glaciers in the high mountains of Huila, Tolima and the Sierra Nevada of Santa Marta will have disappeared by the end of this century. That loss will have a profound impact on the supply of freshwater in Colombia, affecting agriculture, biodiversity and, not least, potable water for Colombia's growing and increasingly urbanized population.

*The Landsat satellite captured these images of Kilimanjaro February 17, 1993 and February 21, 2000 [NASA]*

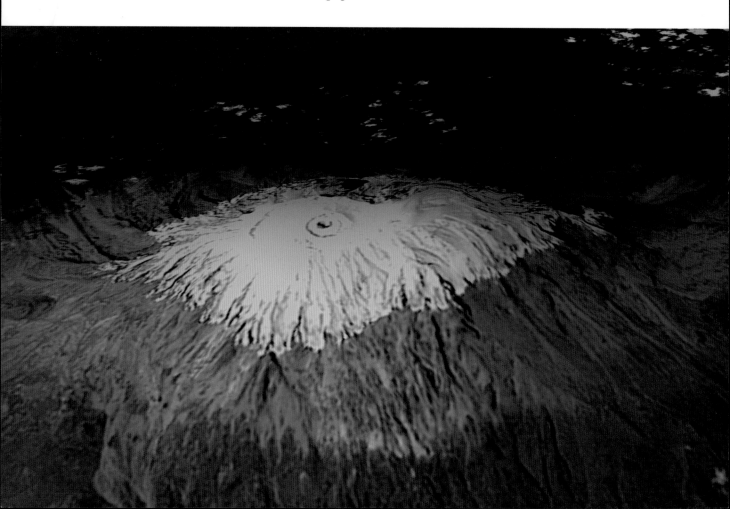

The Colombian Met Office puts the blame fair and square on global warming (*Semana*, March 2005). But is global warming primarily to blame for the loss of the glaciers in the tropics? The short-wave radiation received from the Sun over mountainous regions in the tropics is more than double that over the course of the year compared to mountainous terrain in high latitudes, such as Alaska. For that reason alone the mountains of the tropics need to be considerably higher than their counterparts in the high latitudes before ice will form and settle into a glacier.

The two factors, higher mountains and double the radiation indicate that the potential attrition of ice relative to altitude is much greater than that of a glacier in Alaska, the Swiss Alps, or New Zealand. The tropical mountain needs at least double the precipitation, as snow, to maintain its glacier and snowy peak. Where glaciers have started to recede in the tropics, measurements of atmospheric humidity show a significant drop with a corresponding decline in rainfall.

Soils in the tropics have been drying out over the past fifty years and it is becoming clear that deforestation is playing its

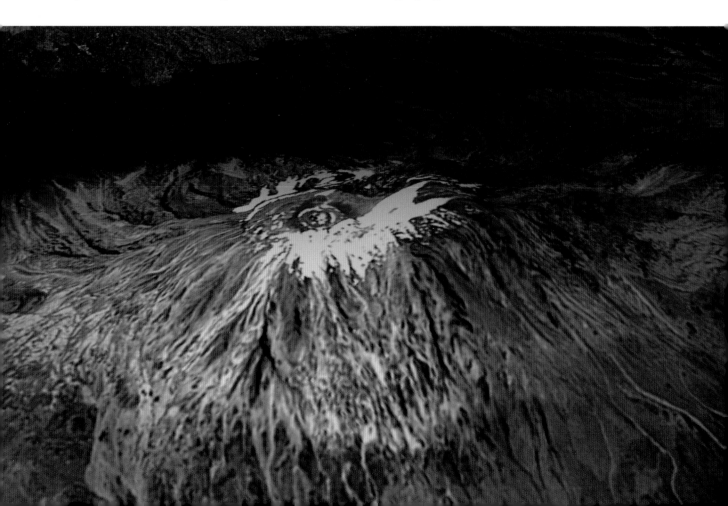

part. In the tropics, the forests, through evapo-transpiration, and through protecting soils help maintain high atmospheric humidity. Is it pure coincidence that the Andean glaciers have vanished at a rate comparable to post-World War Two deforestation in the region? Is there a correlation? Part of the problem in looking for causes is that prevailing wind currents have shifted. Nevertheless, small changes in the convection process result from deforestation, and that means less water vapour and therefore less energy in the system.

Certainly the phenomenon of glacier melt is a global one, regardless of its exact causes. New research from the World Glacier Monitoring Service (WGMS) in Zurich concludes that Europe's Alps, too, are retreating fast, and could lose three-quarters of their extent to climate change during the coming century. According to WGMS data presented at the European Geosciences Union (EGU) annual meeting in Vienna, nearly 4,474 km² of the

*Ice block on a beach near Jökulsárlón, Iceland [Andreas Tille]*

Alps were glaciated in the 1850s. By the 1970s, this had fallen to just under 2,903 km², and in 2000, was only 2,272 km² (BBC News, April 4, 2006).

'From 1850 to the 1970s, there is an average loss of 2.9 percent per decade,' WGMC's Michael Zemp is reported to have told EGU delegates. 'From the 1970s until 2000 it is 8.2 percent per decade, and we see most of that increase since 1985,' he said. Looking ahead, the scientists' projections of such a high degree of glacier loss are based on a rise of 3°C in summer temperatures over the coming century. As glaciers form a natural reservoir of freshwater which is gradually supplied over the summer months, the loss of this water store would seriously affect local populations.

The researchers' computer model shows that even a rise of just 1°C would mean a loss of 40 percent of the glaciated area. And the process of retreat, they say, is already unstoppable because of the temperature rise of the last two decades.

*Ice cave in Franz Josef Glacier, New Zealand [Kym Parry]*

## The Grindelwald rockfall

*Masses of rock falling down from the Eiger Mountain in the Swiss Alps near Grindelwald, Canton of Berne, Switzerland, on July 13, 2006. Around 700,000 cubic metres of stone fell from the Eiger's east face. Geologists have attributed the dramatic fall to glacier retreat and global warming. [Bruono Petroni, PAP]*

On the evening of July 13, 2006, a spectacular mass of rock collapsed from the east face of the Eiger in the vicinity of Grindelwald, in the Swiss Bernese Alps. More than 20 million cubic feet of rock crashed, raising enormous clouds of dust in the valley below, where fortunately, no human dwellings were affected.

Swiss geologist Hans-Rudolph Keusen, the official Swiss monitor of Alpine conditions, had forecast a fall of three times that amount since, from early June onwards, a 16-foot-wide crack had appeared, growing daily until the rockface finally gave way. Scientists have recently warned of the eventual unsheathing of the Eiger's east face as the Lower Grindelwald glacier has retreated in recent years, and only days before, a 100-foot high rock formation also fell away. More falls were expected in the following months.

In a report on *Timesonline,* Keusen pointed his finger at the rise in temperatures resulting from global warming with its effect on the permafrost of the Grindelwald Glacier. Permafrost associated with the glacier is what holds the mountain together, according to Michael Davies, professor at Dundee University and member of the International Permafrost Association. Once the permafrost melts, the resulting water gets trapped inside fissures in the rock and produces cracks which further weaken the structure.

Wilfried Haeberli, geology professor at Zurich University, told the Swiss newspaper *SonntagsZeitung* that the chances of a major disaster occurring have increased as the permafrost melts. Permafrost, which forms above 2,300 metres, binds the rock and soil to the mountain face but this bonding is weakened by rising temperatures. Studies are now under way to identify further areas at risk from similar disintegration of the mountains, especially where towns and mountain resorts may be at risk.

Disastrous rockfalls are nothing new to Switzerland. The village of Derborence, in the Valais region, is famous for having suffered two major falls in 1714 and 1749. The first killed eighteen people, the second, involving 50 million metric tonnes of rock, buried some forty chalets, though some reports say most of the inhabitants escaped in time. A single survivor is reputed to have crawled from the mountain of débris some weeks later. This dramatic event became the centrepiece for the famous 1934 novel, *Derborence,* by the Swiss author Charles Ferdinand Ramuz, and a film of the same name in 1985.

But the most famous and most catastrophic rockfall in Swiss history was that of Goldau in 1806, which killed 457 people and wiped two entire villages off the map. The disaster has been credited with uniting the divided Swiss cantons in a collective wave of support, and hastening the arrival of the Swiss Confederation.

*A woman and a man drink a glass of beer in the mountain restaurant Baeregg above Grindelwald, Switzerland, July 15, 2006, while watching the area at the Eiger Mountain where hundreds of tons of rock were expected to fall. The spectacular mass of rock breaking off the Eiger mountain became an unexpected tourist attraction for the resort of Grindelwald. Hundreds of hikers and hordes of journalists took up position to watch the Eiger slowly shed a large chunk of its eastern flank each day and maybe ponder on what this tells about global warming. [Yoshiko Kusano, PAP]*

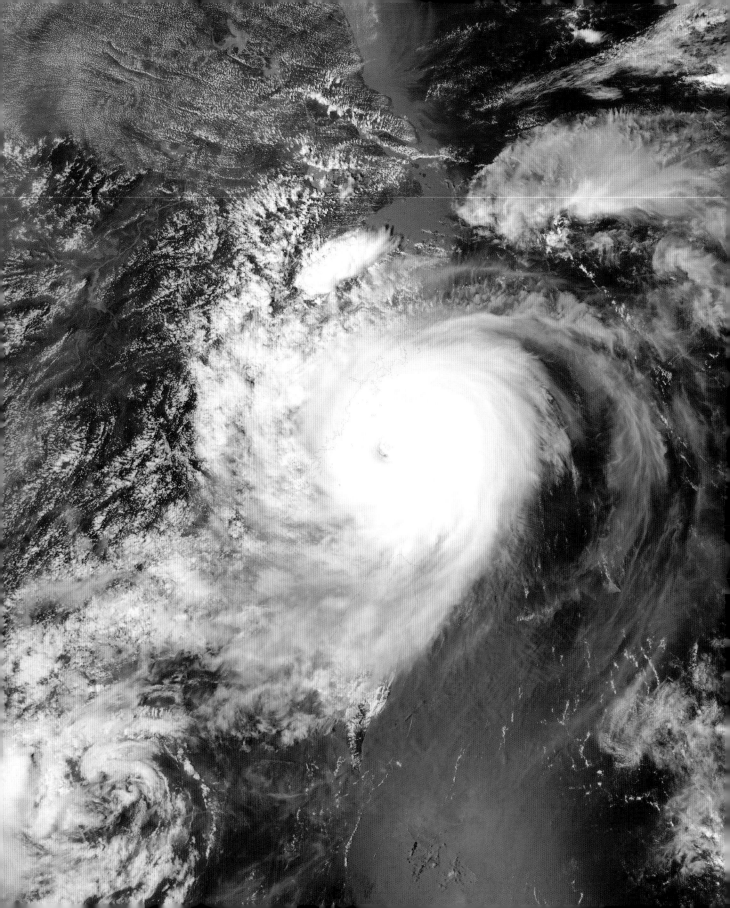

# 4. Floods, Typhoons and Monsoon Winds

## *Floods*

Water is both essential friend and deadly foe; we need it to drink and survive, yet it can kill us. The calm waters of a river flowing gently through our countryside, towns and cities, may bear a beguiling sense of tranquillity, yet, in a flash, that same river can transform itself into a raging torrent that burst banks, destroys houses, sweeps away cars and bears off livestock and people caught up in its path.

Floods are a part of nature: they have always occurred and they will go on occurring. Too often, by not respecting the power of water, we have brought death and destruction upon our own heads;

*OPPOSITE:*
*Typhoon Saomai over China and Taiwan, August 2006  [NASA]*

*BELOW:*
*Villagers from the district of Huachipa try to slow down a mudslide by putting stones on the pavement; February 5, 2002, outside Lima, Peru*
*[La República Newspaper/Getty Images]*

we have built our houses, and sometimes even our towns in flood plains or on slopes vulnerable to land and mudslides.

Often these disasters strike those countries least equipped to deal with them. One of the most horrible events to occur over the past twenty-five years was the mudslide that engulfed the town of Armero in Colombia in November 1985. The mudslide was triggered when the 5,000 metre-high, snow-capped Nevado del Ruiz, in Caldas, warmed up as a result of volcanic activity and sent a stream of débris pouring down its slopes. The lahar killed some 24,000 people, one of the most vivid images sent around the world being of a nine-year old girl, trapped in the mire, who despite heroic attempts to save her, could not be released and died many hours later.

By building dams we hold back water, whether for electricity generation, irrigation and even for flood control, but that control can become a two-edged sword, as in 1975, when Typhoon Nina destroyed over sixty dams in China's Hanan province. The terrible consequences of the dams failing in quick succession was more than 200,000 people dead. And in Spain in 1982 the river Jucar in the province of Valencia swept over a reservoir, breaking its walls and releasing thousands of cubic metres of water in a matter of seconds. Some thirty victims died in that disaster.

The major floods that hit central Europe in 2002 left cities such as Dresden and Prague under several feet of water, as rivers such as the Danube burst their banks and wrought considerable damage to the wonderful heritage of those cities. In Germany, the so-called 'flood of a century' *(Jahrhundertflut)* caused at least 2,260 million euros worth of damage.

Practically the same scale of flooding was repeated during August 2005, havoc being caused in Roumania, Switzerland, Austria and Germany. In Roumania, the floods carried away people and inundated some 1,400 houses in the central part of the country. Bulgaria also suffered floods and perpetual rain, leaving some 14,000 homeless for three months. People had to be evacuated in Switzerland and Germany, and the River Aare burst its banks flooding low-lying parts of the ancient city of Bern. In one area the floodwaters rose 5 metres, reaching the second floor of buildings in their path.

Floods can afflict regions where we do not normally expect such disasters to happen, for instance, Ethiopia, which we tend to associate more with drought than with a surfeit of water. But, as we saw in 2006, in such arid or semi-arid areas where the baked soil does not allow rainfall to penetrate, causing surface run-off, flash floods can be particularly dangerous. It is all too easy to be caught unawares

when crossing a dry riverbed, or *wadi,* under the baking sun of a desert, when far away a torrent of rain has fallen. That water quickly runs off slopes, forms streams and then pours into the erosion-scarred breach in the landscape that is the riverbed. One moment you can be on dry land and the next trapped in swirling waters that vanish into the sun-baked sands almost as quickly as they have come.

St George in Utah, in the United States, enjoys a dry, sunny climate for much of the year. In the distance the mountains shimmer in the warmth of the day. On January 14, 2005, a major storm developed over the mountains, dumping a load of snow and then rain. The run-off overwhelmed the Santa Clara River as it passed through Gunlock, catching the town's inhabitants totally unaware. Water swirled down the river, bursting banks and flooding a wide area. Within moments the torrent of churning, mud-filled waters was eroding riverbanks, eating away at what until that moment had seemed safe land. People watched in horror and amazement as houses that had been located well above the river's normal course were pulled into the river, to vanish without trace, a few wisps of smoke indicating the dying moments of a fire that had been blazing in the hearth. Fortunately, no lives were lost.

As we saw in Chapter 1, storm surges can also result in inland flooding as a result of sea-water piling up against the shoreline and

*Rescue workers bring residents out of the floods in Carlisle, January 2005. Carlisle was completely cut off as severe flooding forced the closure of all routes into the city. Police appealed for help from boat owners in the area because cars were unable to reach the city centre.*
*[John Giles, PAP]*

*Two children are seen in their flooded family home in the Kherbari village in the outskirts of Guwahati city, capital of northeast India's Assam state in July 2004  [PAP]*

preventing the outflow of river water into the ocean. Tsunamis, which are not weather events as such but are usually caused by undersea earthquakes, are equally devastating. The Indian Ocean tsunami of December 26, 2004, resulted from a massive quake on the sea-bed off the west coast of Sumatra. The effects were felt all around the Indian Ocean, from Indonesia to the west coast of India and Sri Lanka, with the result that more than 250,000 people lost their lives, both local fishermen and their families, as well as tourists, as the sea-surge swept in over low-lying land. One result of such a major disaster has been the establishment of tsunami warnings right across the Indian Ocean. The lack of communication between the different regions around the ocean resulted in a far greater loss of life than had a warning system been in place.

Meanwhile, in terms of rainfall, never before had so much rain

fallen within a short time as happened over parts of India during the summer of 2005, with 65 centimetres (26 inches) of monsoon rains (see below) falling in Mumbai over one 24-hour period in late July. The ensuing flooding left more than one thousand people dead, with at least one third of the city under water, electricity cut off for days and the region paralysed. Reports estimated that the lives of some twenty million people were affected.

During May 2006, winds and flooding on a dramatic scale struck different parts of the world simultaneously. Massachusetts suffered a degree of flooding that had not been seen before. Rivers bursting their banks and water spilling in torrents over reservoirs and smashing into buildings below were some of the images flashed around the world. Colombia too suffered exceptional rains, and one of the consequences of waterlogging was that the main pipeline carrying gas to the capital, Bogotá fractured leaving people and restaurants without the resources to cook and prepare food for several days.

*A Roumanian peasant woman, Musuroi Petra, 67, is overwhelmed by emotion as she stands in her destroyed kitchen in the flooded village of Ionel, Johanesfeld, near Timisoara city, Western Roumania, April 30, 2005. Ionel village was completely isolated by water, with the only support for the local people being a small barge and a few motor boats to transport their animals and important belongings to a safer place. Instead of preparing for the Orthodox Easter celebration, peasants were trying to save what waters had spared. [Robert Ghement, PAP]*

## What suffering animals tell us

Eduardo Carrillo, a wildlife ecologist at the
University of Costa Rica, was on a field trip to
Corcovado National Park, with a group of his biology students in November 2005 when he realized that
something was wrong. In just over a mile, the group
found five dead monkeys. Three more were in agony,
emaciated, near death, sitting on the forest floor unable to climb a tree.

*Spider monkey infant*
*[Joel Sartore, Getty Images]*

'I had never seen anything like this,' he said,
'not even when yellow fever swept through monkey

populations in the 1950s.' Dr. Carrillo and his colleagues, as well as government officials, worried they
might have a mini-epidemic on their hands, but tissue
samples from Corcovado spider monkeys — Costa
Rica's most endangered species of monkey — sent
to a laboratory at the University of Texas showed no
evidence of a virus or other pathogen.

The explanation for the animals' poor condition
lay elsewhere. September, October and November of
2005 brought nearly twice the monthly average of
rainfall and unusually low temperatures to many parts
of Costa Rica, especially the Osa Peninsula, which
juts into the Pacific in the south. In fact, Corcovado
averages about 24 inches of rain in September, 31
inches in October and 20 inches in November, while
in 2005 more than 39 inches fell in the park in
September, 59 inches in October, and 41 inches in
November.

Costa Rican researchers believe that the affected
animals starved to death because of a lack of available food sources and an inability to forage for
food during several months of extreme rain and
cold. Some fruit trees did not bear fruit during the
rainy months. Others produced fruit but it fell to the
ground early, leaving nothing on the trees for long
periods of time.

The suspicion is that climate change is at heart
of the unusual wet weather. 'The lesson is that we
should document as much as possible from now on
with this kind of event and try to establish a link
to the climate change process,' commented Carlos
Manuel Rodríguez, the environment and energy
minister, and went on, 'Costa Rica is committed to
reversing the process of climate change,' citing the
country's rainforest preservation efforts, ban on oil
drilling and interest in renewable energy. 'We don't
see the rest of the world doing a good job.'

(Source: Report by Hillary Rosner, *New York Times,*
March 7, 2006.)

*Typhoons*

Typhoons are no less devastating than hurricanes, and their origins are essentially the same. And just as hurricanes in the Caribbean have been stronger and longer lasting in recent years, so too have typhoons. Mid-August, 2006, was certainly something of an extraordinary experience for the Chinese, in a year when China was struck by eight major storms. In a matter of a month, the country experienced three tropical storms, with the unusually violent Typhoon Saomai exceeding all others in strength, even those of recent years, such as Typhoon Ranamim which in August 2004 ravaged Wenling in Zhejiang province.

Saomai was the strongest typhoon to hit China since 1956, with winds of up to 270 kilometres per hour (170 mph). It caused deaths in the Philippines and as it rampaged through Japan, Taiwan and Hong Kong, airlines cancelled hundreds of flights. The official Xinhua News Agency reported that more than 1.6 million people had evacuated before the storm hit China. In its aftermath, almost two hundred people were missing and the coastal city of Wenzhou alone suffered 4.5 billion yuan (USD 560 million) in damage, including more than eighteen thousand flattened houses. The winds and sank more than one thousand fishing boats. Six cities had their electricity cut as cables snapped and pylons toppled in horrendous gusts of wind. In places, about 30 millimetres of rain fell in an hour (12 inches).

Throughout the region, storm shelters collapsed in winds that exceeded any others during the last five decades since records began in 1949. There was better preparation than in 1956, when a typhoon with winds up to 260 kilometres per hour (145 mph) killed some 5,000 people in Zhejiar, mainly as a result of an associated storm surge, and on this occasion, foresight helped keep the death toll down. But the relatively few deaths from Saomai must be put into context, and tropical storm Bilis, that struck China a month earlier, in July, 2006, killed some six hundred people in the same area that was later to experience Typhoon Saomai. In fact, China has experienced an exceptional year for tropical storms and typhoons, with many missing and killed. In addition, typhoons usually never develop so early as they did in the 2006 season. We are seeing another record broken, just like the 2004 hurricane which struck southern Brazil, where hurricanes simply can't happen.

Deluges and floods have always occurred, not least the one suffered by Gilgamesh, more than three thousand years ago, and there is every evidence to suggest that a cataclysmic flood did indeed

affect the cradle of civilization in Mesopotamia around that time, giving rise similarly to the biblical account of Noah and his ark. Climate sceptics, and not just those that read the Bible, will continue to point out that such events are part of natural variability and that we cannot draw conclusions from them of human-induced climate change. Nevertheless, it is clear that something grave is afoot with the world's weather, and the only sensible conclusion is to take seriously the evidence that climate, which gives rise to weather, is changing at a pace that many climatologists had failed to predict.

UK climatologists have been at the forefront for generating climate models that predict unpalatable consequences of climate change. One aspect of such modelling is to show how events in one part of the globe are influenced by events of a distinctly different nature in another part. Could the 2006 season of flooding in the eastern seaboard of the United States have anything to do with deforestation and drought over the Amazon Basin such as was registered in 2005?

*Nanzhen village, Fujian province, southeastern China. Villagers collect their belongings from a house destroyed by Typhoon Saomai on August 14, 2006. The death toll from Typhoon Saomai, the strongest storm to strike China in fifty years, jumped to at least 214, after authorities in Fujian province said the number of fatalities there alone had increased to 125, according to state media.*
*[China Photos/Getty Images]*

Nicola Gedney and Paul Valdes, from the Department of Meteorology, University of Reading, and Bristol University show from their models that, independent of global warming, deforestation of the Amazon could lead to higher levels of rainfall over the north east Atlantic and western Europe, as well as the eastern seaboard of the United States, especially during the northern hemisphere winter months.

Normally, during those winter months, convection is at its strongest over the Amazon Basin. Such convection, based on the lifting of considerable quantities of vapour, then propagates strong Rossby waves some of which head out (teleconnect) in a north-westerly direction across the Atlantic towards West Europe. The Rossby waves emanating from the Amazon tend to be suppressed by strong easterlies aloft; nevertheless, under normal circumstances, with the forest intact, the latent heat source for the Rossby waves is strong enough to override the easterlies. That situation reverses when the forest is replaced by grassland, because of a reduced precipitation over the Basin, which itself leads to a generalized weakening of the tropical air mass circulation — the Walker and Hadley cells. Under those circumstances the easterlies aloft bring about a suppression of the now weakened Rossby waves.

As Gedney and Valdes point out: 'Our results strongly suggest that there is a relatively direct physical link between changes over the deforested region and the climate of the North Atlantic and western Europe. Changes in Amazonian land cover result in less heating of the atmosphere above. This then weakens the local Hadley Circulation resulting in reduced descent and increased rainfall over the south eastern US. The result of this is a modification to the Rossby wave source which causes subsequent changes in the circulation at mid and high latitudes in the northern hemisphere winter. This in turn causes changes in precipitation, namely an increase over the North Atlantic and a suggestion of some change over Western Europe.'

## Monsoon winds

The word monsoon is derived from the Arabic *mausim* meaning 'season,' and was a term used by Arab sailors to describe the winds of the Arabian Sea which generally blow from the north-east for one half of the year, and from the south-west for the other half. Without the annual monsoon winds, the peoples of south-east Asia would want for fresh water and food, yet a huge price is paid in the misery, disease and death that go with the monsoon's torrential rains and the resulting

flooding. Around the Indian sub-continent, the north-easterly winter winds bring dry and pleasant weather, but the summer monsoon season, from June to September, sees rain-carrying winds from the southwest. Most of India's rainfall occurs in that short season, with daily downpours of rain. Both the Indus and the Ganges rivers are liable to flooding, with snowmelt from the Himalayas worsening the problem.

Bangladesh, a young nation founded less than forty years ago, is well known as one of the poorest and most flood-prone nations in the world, with half the country at most 5 metres (13 feet) above sea-level. Fifty-four tributaries and rivers flow into the country, which has the largest system of deltas and flat lands in the world. Virtually every year, large areas are hit by floods as the melting of the snows in the Himalayas combines with monsoon rains and cyclones, and unusual tides in the Bay of Bengal. In 1970 and 1991, tropical cyclones forced storm surges killing some tens of thousands of people. The storm of 1970 produced a storm surge of 9 metres in which houses, crops and hundreds of thousands of livestock were swept away.

*A mother carries her child in one hand and a packet of collected food in the other down a flooded road to her home in Trimohony on the outskirts of Dhaka, August 2002. Floods, an annual disaster for a country criss-crossed by some 230 rivers, caused grief for thousands of people living in the low lying areas around the capital, as well as leaving up to seven million people homeless across the country after severe monsoon rains.* [Jewel Samad, PAP]

In one of the worst episodes in recent history, in 1998, huge areas of all Bangladesh were flooded for two months, leading to two thousand deaths and widespread crop failures, with tens of millions of people made homeless. Around 70 percent of the country and two-thirds of the capital Dhaka were inundated.

July 2004, again, saw some of the worst flooding in decades in Bangladesh as heavy rains as well as surging floodwaters from India and Nepal combined to cause chaos and disruption across some forty of the country's 64 districts. An estimated fourteen million people were affected by the flooding, with over one hundred people killed, a million acres of crops destroyed, a thousand kilometres of roads and highways flooded, and key flood protection embankments damaged.

The outlook is not good for the suffering people of Bangladesh. A further rise in sea-level would be a huge threat to the existence of many people. Given an average relative rise in sea-levels of 4–8 millimetres per year in recent years, this would amount to a rise of 8–16 centimetres within twenty years. Were the sea-level to rise by 45 centimetres, studies anticipate a permanent loss of up to 15,600 square kilometres of land. If sea-levels rise by one metre, 14,000 to 30,000 square kilometres will be permanently flooded, meaning that more than one fifth of Bangladesh will be under water. Because of the high density of the country's population, the number of people affected would be extraordinarily high. In this scenario, 10 to 15 million people could lose their homes. An added loss would be the huge mangrove swamps of the Sundarbans which extend along the coast and, apart from serving as natural storm barriers, provide the ecological systems on which the inhabitants depend for their subsistence and livelihood.

Added to those risks, alarming as they sound in themselves, recent studies, such as the 2005 WWF Global Climate Change report, strongly suggest that deforestation as well as accelerating glacier meltdown in the Himalayas will lead to an increased risk of flooding in years to come in India's river plains, as well as in China and Nepal (see also Chapter 3), to be followed by years of drought as the precious water supply source of the glaciers disappears. The WWF warns that hundreds of millions of inhabitants of the subcontinent could be affected.

In fact, all tropical land masses, northern Australia, Africa, South America and even the USA, experience the equivalent of a monsoon, while the most prominent winds affect south-east Asia. On account of the Earth's tilt and its trajectory around the sun during the course

*The 1998 floods in the Swifts Creek valley in Victoria, Australia, were the largest experienced in the region. The image on the left shows the Swifts Creek bursting its banks at a depth of approximately 4 metres (compared to usual flow of half a metre). The image above shows the same location eight years later, in June 2006.* [Peter Firus]

*A thunderstorm moving into Swifts Creek, Victoria, Australia, February 2006 [Peter Firus]*

of the year, the equatorial belt that receives most solar energy shifts between the two tropics. When the sun is overhead, it heats up the continents faster than it does the ocean. The resulting convection draws the humid air mass in from the warm ocean, whether it be the Indian Ocean or the tropical Atlantic, pulling the air circulation across the equator to the north during the northern summer and vice versa to the south during the southern summer. On reaching land the convection upwards of the air mass and its resulting cooling leads to heavy rains. The Indian summer monsoon is affected by the Himalayas, which act as a barrier and force the air upwards, just as the Andes do in South America, so intensifying the upwards convection. Land masses which traverse the equator and hence experience two summer periods, such as Indonesia, get two monsoon seasons, whereas India just gets the one. The double monsoon makes south-east Asia one of the most fertile regions in the world.

The monsoon over Brazil and the Amazon Basin takes place mostly during the northern hemisphere winter. During that period the ITCZ (the intertropical convergent zone that draws the trade winds together over the land mass) moves southwards to fill the vacuum left by the convection of warm humid air upwards. That motion of the air mass — of the Hadley Circulation — draws air in southwards from the warm tropical Atlantic Ocean. Conversely, during the northern summer, the ITCZ gets drawn further to the north and the rains may fall nearer the continent's Caribbean coast.

## Monsoons and pollution

Climatologists have assumed for some time that global warming would cause the Indian Ocean to warm up and lead to stronger monsoon rains. At least, that is what their models predicted. However, as Veerabhadran Ramanathan and his colleague Chul Eddy Cung of the Scripps Institute in La Jolla, California, have discovered, the opposite appears to be happening. They have now corrected their models to take account of the brown haze of pollution that covers much of northern India and the Indian Ocean and they find that whereas equatorial regions of ocean have warmed, the same is not true of the higher latitude Indian Ocean. In the *Journal of Climate* (vol. 19, p.2036) they report that the pollution is preventing sunlight from reaching the ocean surface and has changed what should be the normal summer temperature gradient and is therefore causing the monsoon rains to move south and fail to meet land. Their model now predicts that rainfall over the Indian sub-continent should fall rather than increase. That fits in with the facts; rainfall has declined by between 5 and 8 percent since the 1950s.

# 5. Where Have All the Rainforests Gone?

## *The worldwide destruction of rainforest*

Practically every year, during the months of August and September, people in Indonesia and Malaysia suffer from the burning of Kalimantan's forests to make way for African oil palm and rice. Smog causes schools to shut down, planes are unable to land, visibility is down to the width of a street. One might have thought that such life-threatening pollution would have given rise to violent demonstrations, that people would have worried about the loss of the ecological services provided by the forest, including its impact on regional weather, but not so: people remain passive, accepting the annual destruction of the ancient rainforests of Borneo as an inevitable consequence of Indonesia's economic development. The Indonesian government has just announced that 30,000 hectares of forest in a national park are to be cleared for the oil palm: that is 15 percent of the total park area. Soon there will be simply nowhere for the orangutan to go, except to languish in some zoo.

The irony is that just a handful of people get rich from the destruction, most of them big plantation owners and when small farmers are implicated it is as a result of government schemes, such as that of President Suharto in the 1990s, with his million hectare Mega Rice Project. The forest was destroyed, the peat drained, so making it vulnerable to fires. The construction of the trans-Kalimantan highway clinched the destruction in allowing settlers access to the heart of the forest.

Some years the burning is worse than others, as during a strong El Niño event such as occurred in 1997 to 1998, and then again in 2002 to 2003. In the first of the two events, 12 million hectares of forest, scrub and grassland were set alight, the smog from the fires covering an area that encompassed parts of Malaysia, Sumatra, Kalimantan and Singapore. With eyes smarting, throats burning and the inevitable inhalation of smoke particles, millions of people were badly affected, especially in areas of high population density such as Singapore. Just for adverse health effects alone, the costs of the fires have been put at USD 3,000 million. Add to that the release of greenhouse gases, and Indonesia was responsible that year for emitting as much as one third of all the world's emissions.

*OPPOSITE:*
*Brazil: slash and burn rainforest clearance. Large swathes of rainforest are destroyed to make way for commercial cattle ranching.*
*[Jacques Jangoux, Getty Images]*

*NEXT PAGE:*
*Dusk, Amazon Basin, Brazil, June 2001 [Marcus Lyon, Getty Images]*

*A mother and child watch the flames creep towards their house, March 16, 1998, near Balikpapan, Indonesia. The arrival of an early dry season resulted in fires raging in the East Kalimantan region of Borneo causing an estimated 200 million dollars in damage.*
*[Paula Bronstein/Liaison/Getty Images]*

With the forest intact, the dry conditions of an El Niño year do not necessarily of themselves lead to fires and uncontrolled burning. But, add in the damage done to the forest by loggers, and it takes one spark, one lightning strike, to set abandoned branches and brushwood ablaze. The situation in Kalimantan is made considerably worse because of extensive peat bogs in the central and eastern part of the country that, once alight, cannot easily be extinguished.

In Africa, tropical rainforests are equally under attack. In Congo Basin countries such as Cameroon, Congo and Gabon, logging is the huge threat; it is estimated that, every year, 137,000 hectares are logged in those three countries alone. Although loggers often only take the few most valuable trees, leaving others behind, the 'selective' removal of trees can be very damaging to the remaining forest. One hectare of rainforest has to be felled to log just one mahogany tree, and, where logging roads go, people usually follow. The roads themselves may not cause massive deforestation, but the settlements and farms that follow in its wake often do.

Some areas of rainforest are rich in minerals, including oil, gold, aluminium, iron and cobalt. Seismic testing for oil disturbs wildlife and, as with the logging industry, the cutting of tracks and routes for oil pipelines or for access to mines simultaneously opens up routes into the forest for people wishing to occupy and clear the land for farming. An ensuing major cause of forest loss therefore is clearance for commercial and subsistence farming. Huge plantations of rubber trees, banana and African oil palm now stand where rainforests once grew.

Not even the world's richest rainforests are immune from attack, and the Pacific Coast forests of the Choco in Colombia, are being felled, mostly illegally for plantation crops, exploited for the most part by Colombia's paramilitaries. They, together with their implacable enemies, the Revolutionary Armed Forces of Colombia (FARC) also thrive from the production of coca and cocaine in Colombia's Amazon, with the paramilitaries gaining as much as 75 percent of their incomes from illicit crops.

Government spraying of the coca and poppies, using concentrations of herbicides that would never be permitted in the USA, is funded by the United States. The sad truth is that the spraying with Round-up not only destroys crops and trees, some indeed legitimate and part of subsistence living, but it leads inexorably to the destruction of more forest as the colonist peasants move deeper into the jungle in the bitter battle to survive. Nowhere in the government is there a proper sense of the immense loss of species, a multitude as yet unknown, or any recognition that the wettest forests in the world, with 40 feet or more in rainfall each year, are dependent for rainfall patterns that are generated by the very same forests themselves.

## The decline of the Amazonian rainforest

Going back at least forty years, Brazil has unleashed a process of development in its Amazon Basin that is leaving vast areas shorn of trees. A combination of satellite imagery and verification on the ground suggests that, by 1998, the area of forest cleared in the Brazilian Amazon had reached some 549,000 square kilometres, hence about the size of France out of a total area as large as Western Europe. In no more than a few decades, Brazil has managed to deforest an area far greater than that lost over the preceding five centuries of European colonization.

And the destruction has continued. In 2003 an area the size of Belgium was cleared, some 23,750 square kilometres, two percent up on the deforestation of 2002. In 2004, remote satellite sensing picked up more than thirty-five thousand separate fires in the Brazilian Amazon, an appalling figure that was still surpassed by double in 2005, in great measure because of forest fires caused by the drought.

Governments and corporations tend to blame rainforest destruction on the actions of subsistence farmers and settlers. Subsistence farmers too often have little idea how to farm in the heart of the tropics, where soils are often fragile and depleted of nutrients. For lack of opportunity, such colonists may be forced to occupy the least fertile areas, where their actions rapidly deplete the soil. The net result is a cancer-like need to clear more forest, just for subsistence.

However, government schemes themselves have deliberately encouraged the 'colonization' of rainforests and, throughout the tropics, small-scale farmers have been forced off their own lands and into poorer forest areas by large agricultural companies, as during the 1970s and 80s when small-scale tenant farmers had to leave the rich fertile lands of Rio Grande do Sul in the southern part of Brazil.

International development agencies, such as the World Bank and the European Commission have, in the past, funded projects such as resettlement schemes, roads and dams, all of which have led secondarily to the destruction of rainforest. Reaction against such 'funded' destruction has altered the ethos of such organizations, which now incorporate policies that supposedly protect the environment. In the main, those same organizations take very little account, if any, of the association between climate and tropical rainforests. That lack of concern is a great failing.

For all the talk, how well those policies work in practice is a moot point. GTZ, Germany's overseas aid agency for tropical countries is building a road in Alto Amazonas in Peru that will undoubtedly destroy the last vestiges of forest in an area that has been developed for paddy rice production. The purpose of the road is to cut directly through land that is currently circumvented by the Mayo River, so shortening transport time by several days.

*Illegal timber extraction*
Multinational timber companies, particularly from Malaysia and Indonesia, have entered the Amazon in a big way. In 1996 alone Asian companies invested more than USD 500 million in the

Brazilian timber industry. They now own or control about 4.5 million hectares of the Brazilian Amazon, according to Brazil's national environment agency, IBAMA. Meanwhile, in 1997 Greenpeace International investigated the Brazilian trade in mahogany and discovered through tracking with UV visible paints that at least 80 percent was illegally harvested, destination Japan.

The government accepted Greenpeace's findings and in order to combat the poor forestry practices that go with illegal extraction, announced that it would open an additional 14 million hectares of forest in thirty-nine national forests to *bona fide* timber companies, the rationale being that it would therefore be able better to control and regulate logging practices. Meanwhile, Greenpeace estimates that at current rates of logging virtually all the mahogany worth extracting will have been taken in as little as eight years. Recent research indicates that selective logging, even when legal, damages and kills many more trees than the one taken out. For every tree extracted, thirty more trees are damaged and become vulnerable to forest fires.

Marina Silva, Brazil's environment minister, has described how the Government was finally cracking down on the felling by seizing

*This picture released 14 February 2006 by the international environmental group Greenpeace and dated August 2005 shows the BR163 road near Castelo do Sonho in the Para State in Brazil. The BR163 road, created by the Brazilian Government in 1988, cuts through the National Forest and is used for illegal logging operations and deforestation inside a protected area. An area twice the size of Belgium has been given greater protection in the Amazon after a Presidential decree in 2006. The decree, signed by President Lula of Brazil, calls to create a 6.4 million hectare conservation area and for 1.6 million hectares to be permanently protected and totally off limits to logging and deforestation.*

*[Daniel Beltra/AFP/Getty Images]*

*Borneo, April 2005. Logged wood is being transported over the Katingan river from the National Park Sebangau. The tropical rain forest of this island which is divided between Indonesia, Malaysia and Brunei is severely threatened by illegal logging and the cultivation of palm oil plantations. If this exploitation doesn't stop, the forests on Borneo will disappear completely by 2020 according to the World Bank. Forests are crucial for the existence of many rare plants, trees, birds and animals, like the orangutan. [Koen Suyk, PAP]*

illegally cut logs, closing down illicit enterprises and fining and imprisoning offenders. As a result, she says, actual felling of the forest was down by 31 percent in 2005. Even so, it only returned to the levels it was in 2001, still double what it was ten years before. Forest destruction accelerated after the Canadian multinational Cargill built a huge port for soya three years ago at Santarém, all of which encouraged entrepreneurs to expand the area dedicated to growing soya.

Nevertheless, as Antonio Nobre of Brazil's National Institute of Amazonian Research, points out, we may be perilously close to the tipping point when the forest can no longer sustain itself and begins dying back. 'What we had predicted for 2050 appears to have begun to take place in 2005.'

## Deforestation by fires

Bill Laurance, of the Smithsonian Tropical Research Institute in Barro Colorado, Panama, points out that in 1998: 'fires lit by small-scale farmers swept through an estimated 3.4 million hectares of fragmented and natural forest, savanna, regrowth and farmlands in the northern Amazonian state of Roraima. Even in the absence of drought,' he says, 'Amazon forest remnants experience sharply elevated rates of tree mortality and damage, apparently as a result of increased desiccation and wind turbulence near forest edges. These changes lead to a substantial loss of forest biomass, which has been estimated to produce from 3 to 16 million tonnes of carbon emissions per year in the Brazilian Amazon alone. In drought years, the negative effects of fragmentation may well increase.'

Thunderstorms and lightning strikes have been blamed for starting fires. Yet, according to Mark Cochrane of Michigan State University and Daniel Nepstad of the Woods Hole Oceanographic Institute, the chances of fires taking hold in the natural forest as a result of lightning are minimal. Charcoal studies indicate that in lowland tropical rainforests natural fires are rare events, perhaps involving a rotation of hundreds if not thousands of years. According to recent research by Cochrane and Laurance, 'Fire-return intervals of less than ninety years can eliminate rain forest tree species, whereas intervals of less than twenty years may eradicate trees entirely ... Fragmented forests in the eastern Amazon are currently experiencing fire rotations of between seven and fourteen years. Previously burned forests are even more prone to burning, with calculated fire rotations of less than five years.'

The truth is that fires in the Amazon are a consequence of deforestation and land-use change. Indeed, Nepstad and his colleagues find that forests that have been subjected at least once to fires are far more vulnerable to successive fires in terms of tree mortality. Initial fires may cause up to 45 percent mortality in trees over 20 dbh (diameter breast height) and subsequent fires up to 98 percent mortality. Meanwhile, during observations of fires in December 1997 fires in the eastern part of the Amazon, in Tailândia, they found that initial fires led to the immediate release of 15 tonnes of carbon per hectare and recurrent burns, up to 140 tonnes of carbon per hectare.

Successive dry years, such as a succession of El Niño years, will also make the forest extremely vulnerable to drying-out and fires. During the exceedingly strong El Niño of 1998, says Nepstad, one third of Brazil's Amazon rainforest experienced the soil drying out down to 5 metres, close to the limits of water-uptake through the roots. Consequently 3.5 million square kilometres were at risk, with some trees having to pull water up from as deep as 8 metres. During that period of stress, Nepstad noted that tree growth went down practically to zero as evidenced by canopy thinning rather than leaf-shedding. Clearly, the year 2005 must have stressed the rainforest to an unprecedented degree and a succession of years like that would put paid to much of the rainforest that remains after logging and clearance for agro-industry, both activities adding to the stress of Amazon forest ecosystems.

How close are we to that critical point when the forests are no longer widespread and dense enough to sustain their humidity and that of the surrounding air? It may be that we are perilously close in some regions of the Brazilian Amazon, such as the south-west, on the border between Brazil and Bolivia, where rainfall has recently begun to increase. To some that may indicate that deforestation is

*Fires in Sumatra, Indonesia  [NASA]*

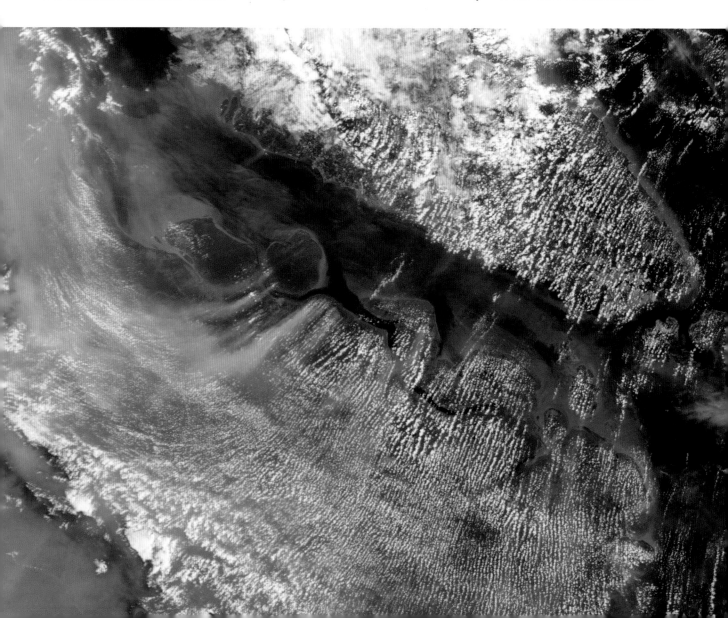

not linked to rainfall: to Roni Avissar of Duke University, North Carolina, such increases spell future disaster and the remaining forest may be in grave danger of collapsing on account of an impending dramatic decline in rainfall (see also Chapter 2).

*Soya — the latest destroyer*

In Brazil, large areas of rainforest have been cleared in order to plant soy beans. As new markets have opened, particularly in the Far East, and in competition with the United States, Brazil has been progressively expanding the land laid down to industrial soybean production. In 1998 Brazil produced about one quarter of the world's soybean harvest, putting it second to the United States which produces approximately half of the global harvest. In 1999, Brazil's land under soya totalled 13 million hectares, therefore more than half the UK's total land surface.

As Philip Fearnside of Brazil's Amazon Research Institute in Manaus points out, soya growing in Brazil spread initially from the states of Paraná and Rio Grande do Sul in the south, to the *cerrado* (savanna) region in Mato Grosso. Meanwhile, all along the way peasants have been displaced, either those in the south who were living off subsistence maize, beans and coffee, or those who had already cleared land in the *cerrado* and parts of the Amazon, as in Rondônia. Since soya production employs only one person on the ground for every eleven subsistence farmers, the peasants have little choice either to move to the city or to move the colonization frontier ever onwards and outwards. In 1996, for instance, Rondônia had 1800 hectares down to soya; in 1998, the area had expanded to 4,700 hectares and one year later to 14,000 hectares. In Maranhâo the soy area increased from 89,100 hectares to 140,000 over the same period.

The ecological impact of soya production, especially in the *cerrado* and Amazonia, is severe. The *cerrado* has biodiversity equivalent to the rainforest, and even more so in the highly vulnerable *ecotone* region twixt forest and savanna. A major concern for environmentalists is the use of agrochemicals for industrial agriculture and soya cultivation in the *várzea* flood plain of the Amazon near to Santarém. During the dry season the area under water shrinks, thereby concentrating the chemicals in soils and wildlife, including fish.

The advancing front of industrial soybean production is unquestionably the leading driver of all the major new transportation projects, including the creation of new highways, the channeling of rivers for navigation, and the construction of new railroads, which will penetrate from the centre of Brazil into the very heart of the

*A Brazilian peasant, member of the Landless Workers Movement, burns transgenic soy seeds during a demonstration before the opening ceremony of the eighth meeting of the Conference of the Parties to the Convention on Biological Diversity (COP 8) in Curitiba, Brazil, 27 March 2006.*
*[Orlando Kissner/AFP/Getty Images]*

Amazon. What is therefore no less than a massive government subsidy has the intention of getting cheap soya transported by ship to Europe, and particularly to Holland for fattening pigs and milk production, and to China, again for livestock production. China, in 2005, signed an accord with Brazil to help develop the infrastructure necessary for the export of Amazon products, such as soya and timber, across the Pacific. Meanwhile the fast-food company McDonald's, as a result of a Greenpeace campaign, has agreed to a two-year moratorium on the purchase of soya as feedstock for chickens, from the Amazon Basin.

But the destruction of rainforest is not just limited to soybean production and the need to get the soya exported out of the country. The very penetration of the Amazon leads to other 'dragging effects' in which more forest is cleared for cattle ranching and for illegal timber extraction than would otherwise occur. Meanwhile, a Dutch agribusiness company is talking of establishing industrial-scale pig farming in the Mato Grosso based on feeding soya. There has been talk, too, of shipping pig manure from the Netherlands to Brazil in the same boats that are now used for exporting soya. And the international chemicals giant Monsanto cannot wait until it gets approval for its Round-up Ready soya; it had expected at least half of Brazil's 13 million hectares would have been transgenic by 2002.

Between 1970 and 1996, the GNP in Brazil's Legal Amazonia, jumped from USD 8.5 billion to USD 53.5 billion, while the population in the region increased from 7.7 million to 18.7 million, a sixfold increase in 'wealth' compared with a 2.4 fold increase in population; but at what cost? In terms of indices of 'human development,' all the Amazonian states had a much poorer showing than was found in the rest of the country, with a large proportion of the local population earning less than the minimal wage. All that can mean only one thing: the wealth generated in Brazil's Amazonia had mostly been exported at the expense of the environment and people.

### Avança Brasil

Avança Brasil is a long-term programme for the supposed economic development of the Amazon Basin. Many are convinced that the programme will have a devastating impact on the remaining forest. Bill Laurance from the Smithsonian Tropical Research Institute in Barro Colorado, Panama, warns that over the next fifteen to twenty years Avança Brasil could accelerate the processes of degradation to the point where more than forty percent of the rainforest will have vanished. Moreover, that left standing will be highly fragmented and vulnerable to further encroachment as well as degradation through 'edge effects' involving increased vulnerability to fires and penetrating winds. Even without Avança Brasil, by 2020, one quarter of Brazil's Amazon forests will have gone at current rates of deforestation.

The intention is to pave about 7,500 kilometres of roads, some new and others currently dirt track. Paved roads are then designated as highways, which, Laurance points out, 'will greatly affect the ease with which loggers, colonists, ranchers and land speculators can gain year-round access to forests, and will lower considerably the costs of transporting timber and other forest products to urban markets. Moreover, highways in the Amazon frequently lead to the spontaneous generation of entire networks of additional roads. For example, the Belém-Brasilia highway — created in the 1960s — is today surrounded by a three to four hundred kilometre-wide swathe of state and local roads as well as logging tracks that has led to a drastic rise in deforestation. Similar networks are evident throughout much of the southern and eastern Amazon.'

## Avança Brasil

Avança Brasil, the Brazilian government's long-term programme for the supposed economic development of the Amazon Basin, has been concerned almost exclusively to date with establishing the infrastructure for the export of millions of tonnes of soya, as well as of minerals and wood. Through a mixture of private and public investment, the plan envisaged as much as USD 228 billions to be spent over eight years, which would lead, according to INPA, the Institute of Amazonian Research, to a rate of forest clearing of between 269,000 and 506,000 hectares per year up until 2020. This 'additional' deforestation would give rise to an increase in carbon greenhouse gas emissions from 52.2 millions of tonnes a year to 98.2 million. Bill Laurance's report (see p.157) claims that all that investment, plus its environmental costs, will result in few local benefits and in poor social participation.

Electricity projects of the past, such as the Tucuruí and Balbina hydroelectric schemes, come under heavy criticism for their failure to meet with expectations, while having a disastrous impact on the surroundings. Balbina, for instance, despite causing the flooding and destruction of around 3,000 square kilometres of forest, is incapable of meeting the electricity needs of nearby Manaus during dry summer seasons. Far from being benign sources of energy with regard to carbon emissions, such hydroelectric plants bring about the release over their lifetimes of at least as much carbon greenhouse gases as from a coal-fired plant generating the same amount of electricity.

*Near Salesópolis, Brazil  [Rodolfo Clix]*

## World weather effects of deforestation

Why shouldn't Brazil, Indonesia, Papua New Guinea or any other country with an inheritance of tropical forests, do what they want with them, just as the United Kingdom or other European countries have been doing over the past few thousand years with their woodlands, conceivably with some impunity?

All tropical rainforests affect weather patterns, either locally or regionally, but the Amazon Basin stands out because of its size and therefore its role in using water captured by the Trade Winds of the tropical Atlantic Ocean to provide essential rain to much of the rest of South America. The corollary, that without the tropical rainforests of the Basin, much of South America would suffer a fearful water shortage, is in all likelihood true. The Amazon Basin is also linked to North America, Europe and South Africa by standing waves of humid air that travel outwards from the Basin in a process described as 'teleconnection.'

Months after winter rains over the rainforests of the Basin, rain brought in by teleconnection gets to the Corn Belt of the United States, just in time for the Spring spurt in growth. Another teleconnection gets rain to South Africa six months after the winter rains over the Amazon. We are beginning to discover just how important the Amazon rainforests are for the world's climate, once we have worked out the time lags between an event somewhere and its consequences months later.

At a meeting in Brazil during July 2006, Dr Antonio Nobre, told of unpublished research that indicated connections between the destruction of Amazon rainforests for timber and agro-industry might be contributing to the spawning of the hurricanes that battered the United States and the Caribbean during 2005. The hot, wet Amazon, he explained, normally sends columns of water vapour into the atmosphere, which rise high into the air, as if in an invisible chimney. That draws in the wet north-east trade winds, which by picking up moisture from the Atlantic leave the surface waters saltier, such that they sink. The net result is that cooler waters from the north move in and help keep down the overall temperature of the tropical ocean. Therefore, it is his conjecture that, by reducing evapo-transpiration over Amazonia, deforestation disrupts the cycle such that the hot water stays on the surface, not only fuelling more hurricanes, but making them stronger.

Climatologists are now discovering just how important the forests of the Amazon Basin are for regulating climate across the

*The River Caquetá flowing through the Putumayo, with its levels way down from the normal. View from a plane.*

## The changing rainforest

The living diversity of the rain-forest can be symbolized by the beauty of its butterflies, their lives intimately connected to the richness of the vegetation. The same vegetation gives rise to moist air currents which feed into global weather patterns. When humans, whether farmers or loggers or developers, come into the rainforest with cattle, cultivation or construction projects, this natural vitality is threatened and in many areas, lost altogether. Instead, we see a dry, scarred landscape, reduced to aridity by overgrazing, and, increasingly in recent years, rivers flowing far beneath their normal levels.

*Cattle, the scourge of rainforests*

*The Tatacoa desert in Colombia, the erosion caused by centuries of cattle grazing. That could be the fate of much of the Amazon Basin were the forests to be replaced by pasture and soya.*

*The drought of 2005 in the Amazon has its ecological consequences. The Geometrid moth (Thyrinteina arnobia) seen laying its eggs in a tea plantation in Ecuador. Large parts of the plantation were totally defoliated.*

*Evapo-transpiration from Amazon rainforests keeps the Hadley air mass circulation going*

*Where will the butterflies be without the rainforest and how will the rainforest survive without the butterfly?*

*[Photographs by Peter Bunyard]*

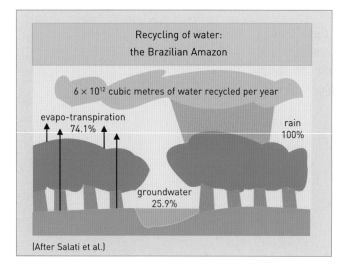

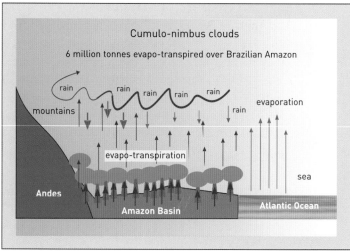

*ABOVE LEFT:*

*The Amazon Basin is a gigantic irreplaceable pump of water vapour and therefore energy*

*ABOVE RIGHT:*

*Up to 75 percent of rainfall is recycled by Amazonian forests through evapotranspiration. In the Brazilian Amazon, no more than 25 percent of rainfall finds its way into the Amazon river. Water vapour carried in the air fuels the Hadley Circulation and therefore helps to drive the trade winds.*

globe. The usual idea of the Amazon Basin is as the lungs of the world, somehow allowing the rest of the world to breathe. But wouldn't savanna or grassland do the job just as well as tropical rainforests and what about the rolling green hills of England? A much better analogy would be that the rainforests of the Amazon Basin are the 'heart' of the world because of all the water vapour and energy that gets pumped out of the region. In fact, tens of times more energy is pumped out than all the energy used by human beings in the world today.

That being the case — that the Amazon Basin is a gigantic irreplaceable pump that gets heat out of the tropics to the higher latitudes — perhaps we should start worrying what will happen to climate if we insist on cutting down great swathes of trees. Certainly, what happened in 2005 throughout the Amazon Basin, not just in Brazil, but in Colombia and Peru, should be a stark warning that we may be close to the limits, if we haven't actually gone beyond them.

During the drought of 1988, caused by a powerful El Niño event in the tropical Pacific, when the normal oceanic currents were overturned, the United States had a foretaste of what would happen were the Amazonian forests to disappear. Corn yields fell by more than a quarter, swallowing up the surpluses of previous years, and for the first time leaving production behind US consumption. The federal government was forced to pay out three billion dollars as debt relief to farmers.

*The Amazon as weather system*

The Amazon Basin, as it is now, has emerged from a tight association of air mass movements and forest-driven evapo-transpiration. In effect, the humid tropical rainforests of the Basin constantly recharge the air flowing above the canopy with water vapour, the net result being that several million square kilometres of forest receive sufficient rainfall for their survival. In addition, just as certain kinds of plankton release cloud-forming substances over the fertile parts of the ocean, so too the trees of the Amazon release volatile chemicals (pungent essential oils such as terpenes and isoprenes) that, on oxidation, form cloud condensation nuclei, which we can often see as a blue haze over a forest. Without such a vapour-cloud regenerating system, those rich forests far to the west of the Basin would in all probability vanish.

The water-transporting mass circulation system of the Hadley Cell begins in the tropical Atlantic Ocean, off the coast of Africa, where dry sinking air travels westwards either side of the equator towards the Brazilian coastline, picking up more and more moisture as it goes. Those Trade Winds, from the two hemispheres, drawn in by updraughts of convecting air over the forest, come together over the equator and finish up moving virtually as one body over the Atlantic forests of Brazil. Through 'convection' they then form giant cumulonimbus thunder clouds that may stretch for several hundred kilometres at a time.

In effect, the process of downpour and then recharging takes place as much as six times as the air mass moves over the Basin, from the Atlantic Ocean and all the way to the Andes. Furthermore, as much as three-quarters of the total volume of water that was originally picked up by the trade winds from the Atlantic Ocean, gets pumped back into the atmosphere, finally leaving the Basin altogether in the mass air circulation that climatologists name as the Hadley Cell after the famous eighteenth century English astronomer. The Brazilian climatologists, Carlos Molion, Carlos Nobre and others, have evidence that as much as fifty percent of the original rainfall gets exported out of the Basin.

Water requires considerable energy to evaporate, some 600 calories per gramme; equally when it condenses and falls as rain that same energy is released as heat and fuels the further expansion of the clouds so that they rise still further, ever releasing more water as rain. Meanwhile, the spin of the Earth — the Coriolis Force — draws the Hadley Cell air mass towards the northeast in the northern hemisphere and its mirror image, hence southeast, in the southern hemisphere. As it loses its water, air mass cools and becomes denser, sinking over East Africa as dry air. Put another way, the deserts of the Sahara and Kalahari are the other side of the coin of the wet, warm air of the Amazon.

This tightly coupled climate system of air currents and forest-driven evapo-transpiration is far more vulnerable to deforestation than we believed twenty years ago. The work of Roni Avissar and Pedro Silva Dias and others (see p.80) indicates that expanding the size of a clearing for agro-industry in the Amazon Basin, at least in the south-western part, will lead to a sharp decline in rainfall and with that the die-back of the surrounding forest. And once the process of die-back begins, like a cancer, it will spread deeper and deeper into the remaining forest as a result of the sun baking down on an ever increasing area. Consequently daytime temperatures over the cleared areas will rise by 10°C or more compared to the forested area.

The forest, as a gigantic irreplaceable water pump, is therefore an essential part of the Hadley mass air circulation system. And it is that system which takes energy in the form of masses of humid air out and away from the Amazon Basin to the higher latitudes, to the more temperate parts of the planet. Argentina, thousands of miles away from the Amazon Basin gets no less than half of its rain, courtesy of the rainforest, a fact that few, if any of the Argentinean landowners are aware of. And in equal ignorance, the United States receives its share of the bounty, particularly over the Midwest.

The system of forest and rainfall may appear to be rugged and therefore resistant to perturbations, but the UK Met Office's Hadley Centre finds otherwise. According to their models, global warming, if uncurbed, will result in a dramatic change in the air mass movement such that it switches from being driven across the Atlantic Ocean by the Trade Winds and hence across the Amazon Basin towards the Andes, to a more El-Niño like pattern, in which the air mass movement passes eastwards across the Pacific Ocean, then to be deflected by the Andes. The net result is a much diminished rainfall regime over the Amazon Basin and the consequences, according to the models, are forest die-back and death, given the vulnerability of the trees to drought-like conditions in successive years. In a matter of decades, decomposition over the Basin may well lead to more than 70 gigatonnes of carbon escaping as carbon dioxide into the atmosphere.

The ultimate result of that drying out may well be desertification of vast areas of the central and western Amazon Basin. But first, we would expect 'savanna-ization' and that is precisely what appears to be happening, as Lucy Hutrya and Steven Wofsy at Harvard have recently discovered. Their discovery indicates that the models of the Amazon rainforests playing a vital role in the hydrology of the Basin are essentially and worryingly correct. In addition, a study of the role of rainforests in keeping the air charged with water vapour over Costa Rica indicates that deforestation is leading to significant reductions in rainfall over the mountains, thus affecting the montane ecology of the region. Changes in hydrology as a result of deforestation within the Amazon Basin will have a massive impact on rainfall patterns over the tropical Andes.

The year 2005 may prove to be a turning point for the Amazon Basin, the signal that the forest may be on the point of vanishing, to be replaced by savanna and even to turn to desert, just like the Tatacoa desert in Colombia, which borders the Amazon, but happens to be in the rain shadow of the Eastern Cordillera of the Andes.

## Rainforest conservation

Conservation bodies, such as the World Wildlife Fund and Conservation International, have understandably focussed on the need to protect regions within the Amazon Basin that are known to be rich in terms of biodiversity. The hope has been expressed that a network of such regions, linked by ecological corridors, would guarantee the survival of as much as 80 percent of biodiversity. Private individuals have also purchased chunks of the Amazon. But such conservation practice is likely to fail in the Amazon Basin for the reason that the rainforest depends on evapo-transpiration in the surrounding forest to provide rain. Consequently, reserves of forest, even when encompassing a million hectares or more, may deteriorate rapidly if the hydrological process is disrupted because of deforestation in bordering areas.

But it's not all bad news and it seems that Brazil, under President Lula, is taking seriously the importance of conserving the Amazon rainforests. He has now given protection to an area twice the size of Belgium, some 6.4 million hectares. That is equivalent to the past three years' deforestation. In fact, Lula's decree calls for around 1.6 million hectares to be permanently protected and off limits to logging and deforestation; another 2.8 million hectares for well-managed,

*According to Roni Avissar's mesoscale research, once the area of forest clearing exceeds a critical point, the remaining forest 'crashes' as a result of a decline in rainfall*

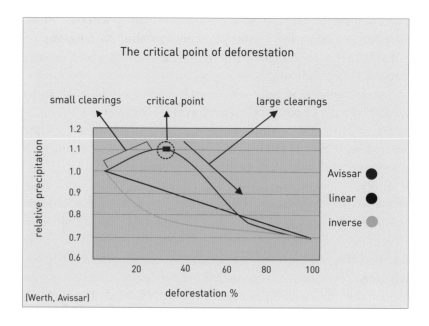

sustainable logging; and the rest for some kind of sustainable development, supposedly some sort of agriculture.

To put the 6.4 million hectares into perspective, it represents less than two percent of the total Brazilian Amazon. The new conservation areas will be created alongside the BR163 highway, which cuts through the heart of the Amazon (see photo p.151). The paving of the road accelerates penetration by colonists and may result in untrammeled deforestation. The hope is that the increased protection will protect the entire area from soya plantations and cattle ranches.

Brazil would lose out terribly were the rainforest to vanish. Currently some 80 percent of Brazil's electricity is generated from hydro-electric turbines. Without the Amazon rainforest to replenish the air mass circulation, the hydrological regime over Brazil would change dramatically, leaving many areas devoid of adequate rain. And if the Amazon Basin were to dry out, as predicted in climatological models, that would reduce substantially the energy currently derived from hydroelectricity.

The impact on Brazilian industry would be immediate, threatening manufacture. In essence, we have a situation where it would clearly be in the best interests of the Brazilian industrial community to do all in its power to protect the Amazon Basin. First and foremost, then, the business community of Brazil and especially the energy sector, must be made aware of the disastrous consequences of losing the rainforests. Self-interest will undoubtedly be more effective in saving the rainforests than appealing to concerns of conservation, however useful and important those may be to protect areas of rich biodiversity.

Much would be gained from the initiatives for protection coming from within Brazil itself rather than from the international community. Once strategies to protect the Amazon are adopted from within Brazil, then international support and help could be invoked without being felt to challenge Brazil's sovereignty.

In recent years, the indigenous peoples of Brazil have been granted title to as much as forty million hectares, an area considerably greater than the United Kingdom. In the 1980s Colombia granted title to its Amazonian peoples, conferring nearly twenty million hectares, and therefore approximately half the total Colombian Amazon. The more land in indigenous hands, even when logging takes place, the better chance for the protection of the whole.

Meanwhile, the rich biodiversity of the Basin needs to be recognized as playing its role in maintaining the ecological fabric of the rainforest. Biodiversity is undoubtedly valuable in itself, but increasingly we are becoming aware that the relationship between tropical forests and climate should be first importance when justifying the need for conservation. Biodiversity conservation then falls naturally in place as the means by which a tropical forest can maintain itself. Providing the means, both in terms of incentives and of enforcement to ensure the conservation of the remaining tropical forests has become a priority. It should have as equal status as concerns over the emissions of greenhouse gases, in the deliberations and recommended actions from bodies such as the Intergovernmental Panel on Climate Change (IPCC).

# 6. Extreme Weather and Climate Forecasting

## *Natural weather variability*

Hot and dry summers, cold and wet winters, rainy springs and bright Indian summer autumns are all part of the natural variability of weather, so how can we actually tease out from background noise the relevant data for forecasting significant changes in climate? That is indeed a challenge and it is only by statistics and the interpretation of such statistics, that we can state with confidence whether something outside the normal is happening.

What about the storm of storms that struck England and Wales in mid-October 1987 and which wrenched some fifteen million trees from the ground, which the UK Met Office failed to predict, even hours before, on account of misreading the information available to them? Can we categorically say that such an event lies outside the normal and therefore shows that climate is changing? Can extremes of weather, as burning heat, bitter cold, days of 'unexpected' torrential rain, or indeed abnormally violent tornadoes and hurricanes, all of which seem to have occurred with increasing regularity throughout 2005 and 2006, tell us anything significant in terms of climate change?

The answer to all that is no, we can't make such assumptions. We would only be able to do so were such severe storms to become so prevalent as to be statistically significant. On the other hand it is increasingly probable that we are on the verge of moving into a new climatic regime. Glaciologists, for instance, are able to date the retreat and expansion of glaciers in the Alps and tropics over thousands of years. Glaciers almost everywhere are on the retreat, nevertheless they are still just within the bounds of variation that has occurred before in the recent past. A couple more years of retreat, as is indeed likely, and yes, we will have passed across into the 'abnormal.' Over tropical Africa, for example, from an expanse of 6.5 square kilometres that covered the high peaks of the Rwenzori Mountains of the Congo and Uganda one century ago, less one square kilometre of ice remains. Higher temperatures, combined with declining precipitation, according to Richard Taylor of University College, London and his colleagues in Uganda, are putting paid to the glaciers, which will be bare of ice in just a few years. As we saw in Chapter 3, an almost similar

*OPPOSITE:*
*October 16, 1987: Storm damage in Soho Square, London*
*[Jim Gray/Keystone/Getty Images]*

outcome is predicted in Europe by the climate model of the World Glacier Monitoring Service (WGMS) in Zurich, which forecasts that over the coming century, the Alps could lose three-quarters of their glaciers.

Statistics obviously depend on the accumulation of data over the spread of time to see whether a trend emerges. Climatologists have agreed to thirty years as being the minimal period of statistical analysis. While thirty years may guarantee that normal variability is taken care of, such methodology suffers a potential defect in that a trend will be discerned in the realm of the abnormal only when it is truly underway; prior to that the data will be averaged and smoothed out. The danger, then, is that climate may have taken us beyond a tipping point, from which it is likely to prove exceedingly difficult to return to the *status quo* of the recent past. At the same time, when we have a spate of warm years, as during the 1990s and 2000s, the hottest ten years for more than a century, climatologists do take note and offer a warning that human induced climate change may already be underway.

## Designing climate models

For the most part, the best we can do with regard to weather, rather than to climate, is to predict a few days in advance and, as the example of the 1987 UK hurricane showed, meteorologists don't always get it right. Massive number-crunching computers, such as those at the UK Met Office in Exeter, have improved the certainty of being close to right some four to five days ahead of actual weather. But climate modelling, predicting one hundred years ahead and using the same basic physics and maths, how can that possibly be acceptable as a projection of climate from today?

For one, modelling climate is not subject to the same constraints as predicting weather, the fine detail matters far less. Global climate models do not pretend to predict, like some Nostradamus, the days in the future when it will or won't rain, whether a hurricane will be spawned on such and such a date. That, for reasons of the non-linearity and chaos in the system would be absurd and no-one would even hazard the attempt. What is important in climate models are the boundaries and constraints in the system on the basis that, from year to year, so much energy is available for distribution from one part of the planet to the other, taking all aspects of climate processes into account.

Global warming assumes, irrespective of what may have brought it about, that more energy from the sun is remaining behind at the Earth's surface. The question then arises how will the energy carriers, be they the air, water vapour, ocean currents, behave in general as global warming from greenhouse gas emissions takes hold. Naturally enough changes in solar input and in the Earth's orbit around the Sun must be predicted and incorporated in the model. Climate sets the conditions which weather systems then act out.

Validation of the models used and whether or not the parameters of the models reflect reality to the best of the model's ability are necessary tools in our having a good degree of well-placed faith in the predictions of climatic conditions. An obvious way to validate the models is to run them backwards from present conditions, to see whether they reflect actual measurements of temperature in the past. Obviously, adjustments have to be made to account for inadequacies in past measurements, all of which requires as exact a knowledge as possible of the methods and apparatus used.

When climatologists run their models back to the starting point of 1870, they look for good correlation with observations and empirical data of 130 years ago. The 'natural' model is intended to represent what has happened over that time until the year 2000, on the assumption that human beings have had no impact on greenhouse gas concentrations in the atmosphere. That natural model proves to be inaccurate, particularly at both ends of the run, overestimating the temperature in the 1870s and underestimating it in the 1990s. In fact, the observations show a 0.6°C rise by the year 2000 compared with the model, a not surprising conclusion since it is such a rise that the IPCC — Intergovernmental Panel on Climate Change — acknowledges as coming from human-induced greenhouse gas emissions.

The next step is to run the model again, but this time to include the accumulations of greenhouse gases in the atmosphere as a result of human activities. Now the fit is considerably better, particularly at the 1870s end of the run. However, the model underestimates the actual warming that took place between 1920 and 1970, even though finishing up reasonably close to the actual average temperatures experienced during the 1990s.

The third experiment involves integrating into the model the main factors associated with climate change, such as variations in

## The evidence from nature

Scientists from seventeen countries across Europe have been studying the ecology of plants and insects to see whether they can detect indications of recent climate change. Observing more than five hundred plant species and a small number of animals, the question was whether, for instance, plants are flowering early and deciduous trees are hanging on to their leaves later, and what impact such changes will have on insect behaviour and the timing of reproduction, dependent as it is on the availability of plant material, at least in the caterpillar and larval stages.

According to a study in the journal *Global Change Biology* (August 25, 2006), the investigating scientists found that spring across Europe arrives six to eight days earlier than in the early 1970s, with warmer temperatures delaying autumn, by an average of three days in the past thirty years. Spain, where early spring temperatures have risen by up to 1°C over ten years, spring is arriving two weeks

*When climate models include the impact of global warming on vegetation, we can see higher temperatures than those predicted in models that do not take carbon feedback into account  [Source: Hadley Centre for Climate Prediction, UK]*

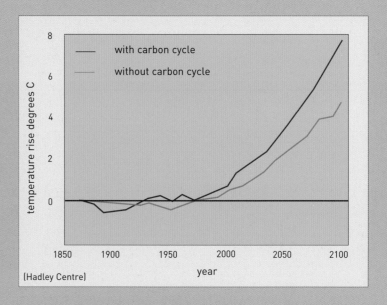

earlier. Britain is warming too, but at a slower rate, with temperatures having crept up by 1°C over the thirty years.

'Not only do we clearly demonstrate change in the timing of seasons, but that change is much stronger in countries that have experienced more warming,' said Tim Sparks, an environmental scientist on the study at the Centre for Ecology and Hydrology at Monks Wood near Huntingdon. Dr Sparks pointed out that natural processes such as pollination were clearly being put at risk from climate warming.

'One of the biggest problems is that species don't adapt to warming at the same rate. So if you have a bird that feeds on an insect that relies on a certain plant for food, and any one of those responds to warming differently to the others, the whole system can break down,' he said.

The study shows that 80 percent of all the species studied are being affected and according to Annette Menzel, a co-author: 'Unlike some studies that record individual species, this is the first comprehensive examination of all available data at a continental scale, using around 550 plant species, and the timing change is clear, very clear.'

The study reveals the impact on nature of fairly modest temperature rises. The impact is strongest on migratory birds that winter in Africa but return to Britain to breed.

'It's as if they're turning up late for a meal, in the middle of the main course, when the starter has gone,' said Dr Sparks to the *Guardian* (August 26, 2006).

Already rare species are the most vulnerable and are likely to get pushed out by common species as they expand their territories. Nevertheless, the loss of some species will be offset by newcomers from mainland Europe.

*A foxglove flowering in November, 2005, in Cornwall, south-west England*
*[Peter Bunyard]*

## Understanding statistical records

Up until 1941, sea-surface temperatures were made through hauling up buckets of water on to the deck and shoving in a thermometer, whereas since then they have been made by measuring the temperature of sea-water at the intake for the ship's engines. In addition, between 1856 and 1910, points out Mark Maslin, of University College, London, canvas buckets were exchanged for wooden buckets, and that affected the amount of water evaporated in the transit from the sea to the deck. Steamers also replaced sailing ships, so altering again the amount of water evaporated, because of the difference in the height of the decks above the sea in each instance.

To obtain reliable comparisons, oceanographers must therefore go back to those early measurements and calibrate them according to modern techniques. When all that is done for land-surface air measurements and for sea-surface temperatures, climatologists find that temperatures have increased by an average $0.65^c \pm 0.05^c$ since the 1870s.

*Wooden bucket  [Sean Okihiro]*

solar input, the cooling effect of aerosols, those sulphur dioxide emissions, for instance, from coal burning. This time the model fits observations considerably better, all of which makes climatologists somewhat more optimistic, that when they run their models into the future rather than into the past, their predictions might hold a little more weight.

Yet, that assumption is also fraught with problems, because it neglects the possibility of tipping points in the dynamic of climate, and the more we know about chaotic systems, such as climate, the more it becomes clear that assumptions made regarding the past and present, however well the models fit, are absolutely no guarantee that the same models will predict the future. One serious omission in the models of the past has been the failure to incorporate the vegetative carbon cycle into the equation. Instead the organic carbon cycle was put into a black box, or rather a physical, unvarying constant, as if climate change had minimal or no impact on life.

Also missing, and equally important, is the impact life has on the forming of clouds that, not only bring essential nutrients from the sea to the land, but bring rain and keep the planet cool. The more scientists delve into cloud-forming activities, the more they find life's ever ubiquitous presence. Life, whether photosynthesizing algae such as the coccolithophores that, in their billions, roam the oceans, whether epiphytic bromeliads clinging on to the great skyscraper trees of the rainforests of Central and South America, or indeed, whether sphagnum moss in the vast expanses of the high latitudes, all release dimethyl sulphide, which on oxidation transforms to cloud forming aerosols of sulphur dioxide. In varying degrees, depending on what kind of forest and where, trees also release cloud-condensation nuclei, such as the terpenes and isoprenes of the Amazon rainforest.

In all, as Stephan Harding points out in his wonderful book, *Animate Earth: Science, Intuition and Gaia*, life on Earth may currently be responsible for forming clouds that cool the Earth overall by 10°C. Climate is clearly affected by the amount of sunlight reaching the Earth's surface and therefore solar flares and the Earth's orbit, whether more or less eccentric, and the tilt and which side is tilted, all play their role in giving the Earth its climate. But life, in its manifest alterations of the Earth's surface and albedo, as well as in its production of cloud-generating chemicals such as dimethyl sulphide and the isoprenes and terpenes, is the manager.

The physics, as far as modelling goes, may be relatively sound, whatever else is lacking in the models. Some evidence of that comes from mesoscale modelling, such as has been developed by Roger Pielke, Roni Avissar, Pedro Silva Dias and others (see p.80). Here, the physics, maths and computing power used to obtain climate predictions for the entire planet are focussed down to relatively small regions of the terrestrial environment, like focussing the sun with a magnifying glass and setting twigs on fire. At the mesoscale the modelling shows itself much closer to weather and to the empirical data of the locality, such as wind flow, temperature, humidity and convection processes than can be gleaned from the GCMs, the general circulation models. Applied, for example, to sections of Rondônia, in the south-west of the Amazon Basin, on the border between Brazil and Bolivia, the mesoscale model is able to repeat fairly accurately the convection process of rising air and the formation of thunderstorm clouds.

GCMs, on the other hand, cannot predict cloud formation because of the high dispersal of the data and therefore low resolution, like reproducing a high-resolution photograph into a newspaper. That may prove to be another defect of the GCMs, the inability at that relatively low level of model resolution to determine whether cloud coverage over a specific region of the planet will be cooling or warming.

Clouds undoubtedly shield the surface, as we all know when the Sun flickers and disappears behind a bank of clouds, only to give us back its warmth when it reappears. At the same time, after a warm, sunlit day, if clouds form in the evening, they will hold back the warmth rather than allowing it to dissipate into the sky, as happens during a starlit night. That dynamic between cooling and blanketing the heat of the day makes a profound difference to the outcome of climate and the formation of weather systems — and at the global scale, as opposed to the mesoscale, we just don't know which will predominate, the cooling or the heating. What can be predicted is that a warmer surface, especially over the ocean, will push more water vapour into the atmosphere and water vapour, given the right conditions and in particular the hand of life, will form clouds. The obvious response is that more clouds translate into more cooling and therefore to some degree balance out the heating impact of rising greenhouse gas concentrations. Yet, warmer clouds rise higher and therefore their ability to hold back surface heat is diminished. Does that mean that global warming will add to more warming, by sending clouds higher?

## Life and the atmosphere

As it happens all the major gases in the atmosphere are recycled by life. Nitrogen is recycled by nitrogen fixers and then returned by denitrifiers, all of which are bacteria. Carbon dioxide is drawn into the chloroplasts of vegetation in the biosynthesis of carbohydrates, the net result being the emission of oxygen. The vast majority of organisms need that oxygen for their metabolism, so as to extract the energy embodied in carbohydrates. Burning those carbohydrates returns the $CO_2$.

Methane, for the most part, is generated by bacteria living under conditions (anoxic) where there is a lack of oxygen. Meanwhile, strong ultraviolet light (UVC) passing through the stratosphere splits oxygen into its constituent atoms. Ozone ($O_3$) forms through one of the dissociated atoms interacting with oxygen ($O_2$). A less strong form of ultraviolet (UVB) then breaks down the ozone and so the cycle continues. Without question, the atmosphere, with its current concentrations of greenhouse gases, which so happen to have been 'right' for human civilizations and the development of agriculture, is a phenomenon of life's interaction with the material surface of the planet.

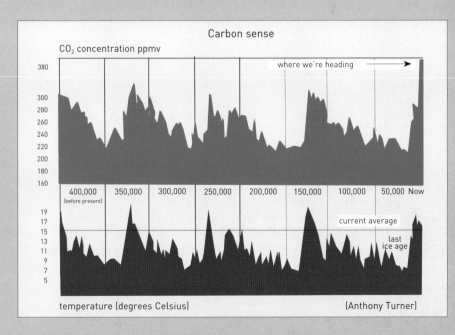

*Throughout geological history, the Earth's surface temperature has gone in tandem with carbon dioxide concentrations in the atmosphere*

Since, aside from water vapour, the most important greenhouse gases in the atmosphere are carbon dioxide, methane and nitrous oxide, life clearly plays a prominent role in the planet's surface temperature. We are now putting back that carbon dioxide until now stored as fossil fuels, such as coal, petroleum or natural gas. We have also cleared forests, on a scale like never before in human history. Soils as well as biomass in the form of trees are venting $CO_2$ and methane. The physics of greenhouse gases tells us that such emissions must bring about global warming. On that score, we can be pretty certain that the 0.6°C rise in average surface temperatures that the Earth has experienced over the last fifty years is a result of our emissions of some 6 or 7 thousand million tonnes ($10^9$ or giga-tonnes) a year of carbon-based greenhouse gases, such as carbon dioxide and methane. In fact, since the start of the industrial revolution we have added 160 giga-tonnes of carbon (GtC) in the form of greenhouse gases to the atmosphere. Together, the greenhouse gases, carbon dioxide, methane and nitrous oxide have added just over 2 Watts per metre squared since pre-industrial times. That heating must be put into the perspective that on average the Earth receives 342 Watts per metre squared.

*Soils and vegetation have been storing carbon for millennia. The Hadley Centre model predicts that global warming will cause a dramatic release of stored carbon over the next century, thus accelerating the greenhouse effect.*

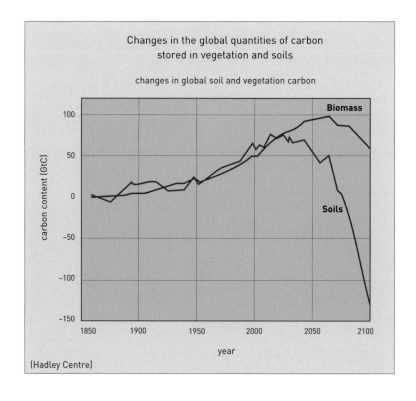

## The price of industrial development

China's rapid industrial growth is polluting the skies over California, with the US Environmental Protection Agency (EPA) estimating that, on some days, nearly one quarter of the particulate matter in the skies above Los Angeles can be traced to China. About a third of the Asian pollution is dust, the result of increasing drought and deforestation. The rest is composed of sulphur, soot and trace metals from the burning of coal, diesel and other fossil

*Beijingers fight against a roaring duststorm as they cycle home after work, March 21, 2001. China's environment is still reeling from years of developmental mistakes with pollution and erosion bound to get worse before the situation gets better, according to a leading environmental official. [PAP]*

*China is currently the world's second
largest emitter of greenhouse gases,
and will soon become the world
number one. China's rapid industrial
growth is already polluting the skies
over California.*

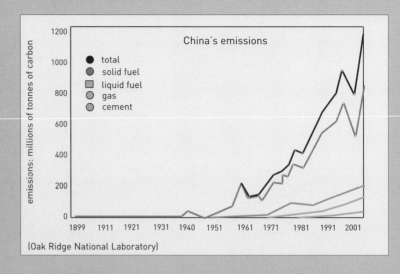

[Oak Ridge National Laboratory]

fuels. The World Bank estimates that most of the world's twenty most polluted cities are to be found in China, where air pollution can be blamed for about 400,000 premature deaths a year. China on average builds a new coal-fired power plant every week and the growth in the economy has resulted in a surge in private cars, adding to the pollution and emissions of greenhouse gases.

Chinese environmental officials warn that pollution levels could quadruple over the next fifteen years if the country doesn't curb energy use and emissions. Beijing plans to spend 162 billion US dollars on environmental clean-up over the next five years, including action to reduce its energy use and air pollution. Beijing has set ambitious goals for increasing energy efficiency, fuel economy standards and use of renewable power sources such as wind and solar power.

*[Stefan Prins]*

## The Earth as weather system

Weather is a momentary, chaotic expression of the forces that determine climate. As the climate changes so weather changes too, rather like a golfer having to adapt to very different conditions, whether on the same golf course, or on other golf courses. And if climate changes dramatically, as it does in emerging from or into an ice age, then weather will change dramatically too. It therefore becomes important to get a handle on the factors that determine climate, especially now that we are almost routinely experiencing new climate-related records, such as the UK's July heatwave in 2006.

What are those factors? First and foremost is the energy received from the sun in the form of short wave electromagnetic radiation, ranging through the light spectrum and beyond, whether in the ultraviolet zone or, at the other extreme, infrared. Nor is the sun a constant, unvarying emitter of energy. Sunspot cycles will have their impact on the radiation emitted, as will the ageing of the sun, for as the sun gets older it becomes more luminous and increases its emissions of short wave electromagnetic radiation. The sun is now estimated to be around one third more luminous than it was some 4,500 million years ago, and were the earth a black body and

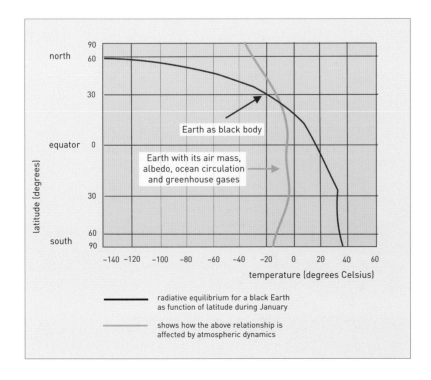

*Climate processes (air and ocean circulation) lead to the Sun's energy getting distributed from the equator to the poles. Without such dynamic movements, winter temperatures over the Arctic would plummet well below –100°C, and summer temperatures would soar to 40°C or more.*

a simple receptor of solar energy, its surface temperature would be considerably higher than it is.

But the Earth is not a black body, nor does it follow a rigid course around an immutable sun. Shortly after its formation, from swirling cosmic gases, the Earth was struck by a planetesimal body the size of Mars. The big 'splat' gave rise to the moon and to the tilt of the now enlarged Earth and so, instead of tumbling over itself like a hurled cricket ball, which is the fate of Mars, the Earth spins in an anti-clockwise direction, as if it were a top. And, like a spinning top that has lost some of its momentum, the angle of tilt varies over a period of some forty thousand years: equally, every twenty-five thousand years or so, the Earth tilts the other way, in what is known as axial precession. Add to that, the Earth moving between a more elliptical to a more circular orbit around the sun, over a period of approximately one hundred thousand years, and we have complex variations in the amount of sunlight being received by the north and south hemispheres of the Earth and in which season. Certainly the combination of those variations appears to have considerable influence as to when

*The Earth's trajectory around the Sun over time affects the amount of sunlight received in the north and south hemispheres*

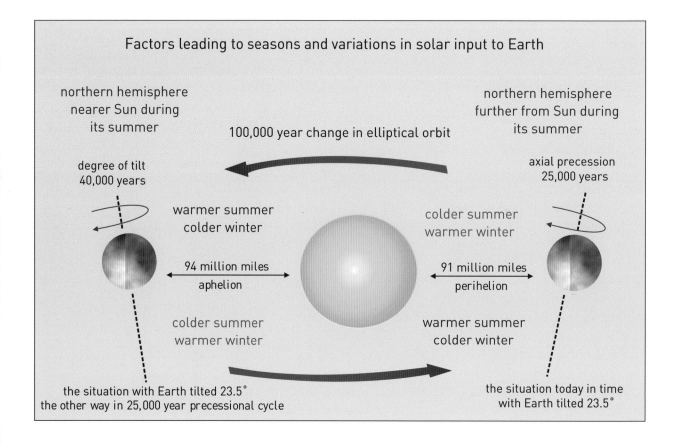

Factors leading to seasons and variations in solar input to Earth

northern hemisphere nearer Sun during its summer

northern hemisphere further from Sun during its summer

100,000 year change in elliptical orbit

degree of tilt 40,000 years

axial precession 25,000 years

warmer summer colder winter

colder summer warmer winter

94 million miles aphelion

91 million miles perihelion

colder summer warmer winter

warmer summer colder winter

the situation with Earth tilted 23.5° the other way in 25,000 year precessional cycle

the situation today in time with Earth tilted 23.5°

the Earth plunges into ice ages or emerges from then. All else being equal, and on the basis of the Earth's wobbles and irregular orbit, we should be heading for another ice age, even if in a few thousand years to come.

But the input of solar energy is not the whole story, despite the opinion of some sceptics who disparage the notion that puny human beings, or indeed life in general, could bring about climate change. The colouring of the Earth is another important factor — what is termed the Earth's 'albedo' (see also Chapter 7). Clouds, ice and snow have high albedo and therefore reflect much of the incoming sunlight, while oceans under clear skies, vegetation and bare rocks have lower albedo and absorb light. Variations in albedo will therefore bring about differential warming or cooling of the Earth's surface, leading to air mass convection, with winds that transport water vapour from one part of the planet to another. In particular water vapour acts as a major means of exporting energy rapidly from the equator to higher latitudes.

Greenhouse gases play their part, mainly carbon dioxide, methane, nitrous oxide and water vapour, and were the Earth to be without them, the average temperature would be some 33°C cooler, not exactly comfortable for mainstream life. Atmospheric water vapour is the most significant of the greenhouse gases, but its presence depends largely on the warmth of surface air as it passes over the ocean. A minuscule 0.001 percent of the planet's water is in the atmosphere at any one time — therefore no more than ten days' supply and just enough if sprinkled everywhere to give each place on Earth 25 millimetres (mm) of rain. But water vapour is not distributed evenly: during the summer months over southern Asia, the air column may contain as much as 60 mm of water compared with less than 10 mm over tropical deserts. In the winter months over high latitudes some air may be virtually dry and contain no more than one millimetre. Other places and at other times may get buckets of rain: on the island of Réunion during March 1952, a total of 1,870 mm of rain fell in twenty-four hours. Obviously, the varied distribution of water vapour and its role in effecting air mass convection results in differential heating of the atmosphere and enhances lower atmospheric turbulence.

Finally, as we have seen, life plays a major 'unconscious' and unintended part in modifying energy distribution and therefore climate and local weather. Life has had a profound impact on the gases in the atmosphere in particular nitrogen, carbon dioxide and oxygen. If it were not for life, the Earth's atmosphere would be mostly carbon dioxide, with an atmospheric pressure sixty times that of today. That would mean the atmosphere would have 150,000 times more carbon dioxide than it has. Where has it all gone? Some gets washed out as carbonic acid, which, through weathering rocks and exposed surfaces, transforms into calcium bicarbonate and limestone that slowly gets washed down to the sea. There, miniscule organisms use the calcium carbonate to make their shells and it is the accumulation over millions of years of plankton that gives rise to formations such as the white cliffs of Dover. Lucky for life, and for us that carbon dioxide has been solidified in this way, so preventing the Earth from overheating.

Photosynthesis, beginning more than three thousand million years ago, is the key to the gradual disappearance of the gas from the atmosphere. Photosynthesis on land and in the ocean, all of biological origin, alone draws down 15 percent of all the carbon dioxide in the atmosphere each year; respiration by all living creatures puts it back again, thus maintaining an overall equilibrium.

When we think of the vast expanses of forests that have dominated the tropics and much of the rest of the land surface since the Carboniferous times some three hundred million years ago, it is not so surprising that the landmass now equals the oceans in terms of net photosynthesis. One way we can measure the success of life is how much the concentration of carbon dioxide in the atmosphere has diminished from more than 3,500 million years ago, with the evolution of blue-green bacteria, the cyanobacteria. The same bacteria are the ancestors of the chloroplasts that in their countless millions can be found associated with the stomata of vegetation — the pores in the leaves of plants.

The sun, as a main sequence star, is gradually becoming more luminous. Astrophysicists estimate that the sun is now 30 percent more luminous than it was when the Earth came into being as a planet some 4,500 million years ago. Luminosity translates into short wave electromagnetic radiation, or sunlight as perceived on Earth, and therefore the Earth should be getting hotter, but on the contrary it has cooled. And we now know the reason: life through several thousand million years of photosynthesis has brought concentrations of $CO_2$ down to the levels we experience today, even if they are beginning to rise again as a result of our hunger for the planet's natural resources.

So the evolution of human beings may well have coincided with the lowest carbon dioxide concentrations ever, namely some 265 parts per million by volume in the atmosphere. Indeed, temperatures have fallen by more than 7°C over the past one hundred million years, leading to permanent ice-sheets in the Arctic Circle and Antarctica, as well as to periods of extensive glaciation followed by melting. At least with a colder Earth, humans have had more land to exploit, more resources to hand, than when sea-levels were as high as they were forty million years ago. Today, some thirty percent of our food is grown in the fertile coastal plains a metre or so above sea-level, therefore making essential food supplies vulnerable to global warming and the thermal expansion of the sea, let alone the melting of glaciers in Greenland and Antarctica.

Scientists debate when the Earth should experience a new ice age. In the 1960s they thought it was around the corner. Now it seems, under normal circumstances we wouldn't experience another ice age for five thousand years. Yet, because of humankind's impact on climate and by doubling carbon dioxide concentrations from pre-industrial times, we could delay such a happening for as long as forty-five thousand years. That would spell disaster, inasmuch as the Earth would return to conditions similar to those of a past age when the ice-caps of Antarctica and Greenland had melted. Under those circumstances, human survival would be seriously threatened, as would much of the Earth's current biodiversity.

## Greenhouse gases and global warming

Jean-Baptiste Fourier was the first to suggest in 1827 that the Earth's atmosphere behaved like the glass of a greenhouse, trapping heat below it. In 1860 John Tyndall measured the extent to which carbon dioxide and water vapour absorbed long wave radiation. Astonished at the apparent power of certain gases to heat up the atmosphere, Tyndall argued that fluctuations in atmospheric concentrations of carbon dioxide might be responsible for recently discovered changes in climate between ice ages and inter-glacials. In 1896, Svante Arrhenius concluded that doubling the atmospheric carbon dioxide concentration, as it was then, would lead to a global warming of as much as 6°C. Fifty years later, in 1940, the British physicist, G.S. Callendar corroborated Arrhenius' calculations by estimating global warming brought about through carbon emissions from burning fossil fuel. It is interesting to see how close, when compared to the latest climate models from the UK's Hadley Centre in Exeter, Arrhenius was to estimating correctly the

## The role of the Amazon rainforest

Cloud formation, humidity and rain, are some of the wonderful attributes that all forests give us, but in particular those tropical humid rainforests that cover some 5 million square kilometres over the Amazon. Through the combined process of evaporation and transpiration, the forest, over the Legal Amazon of Brazil, puts back into the atmosphere more than 6 million million ($10^{12}$ or tera) tonnes of water vapour every year. That is an immense amount in energy terms, equivalent to several million atomic bombs a day, which, without the forest, simply would not be available to the convection system.

And were the forest to decay and die, decomposition would add to the damage by exhaling a considerable quantity of carbon dioxide and methane into the atmosphere, so adding to the rising levels of greenhouse gases. As we saw in Chapter 5, the mesos-cale models of Avissar and Silva Dias show that once clearings have surpassed a certain size, then the processes of convection suck dry the surrounding forest, which in time will die, and leave the region increasingly desertified.

Such a collapse is an attribute of physical processes that depend on a certain density of components for a particular char-

*Colombia  [Peter Bunyard]*

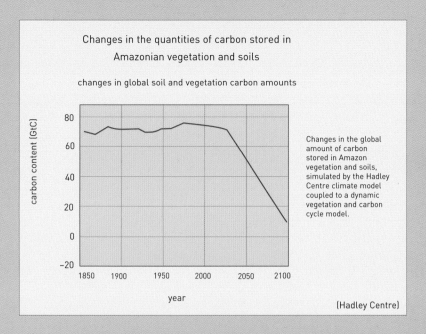

Changes in the quantities of carbon stored in
Amazonian vegetation and soils

changes in global soil and vegetation carbon amounts

Changes in the global amount of carbon stored in Amazon vegetation and soils, simulated by the Hadley Centre climate model coupled to a dynamic vegetation and carbon cycle model.

(Hadley Centre)

*If the Amazon rainforest goes, we could see a massive loss of stored carbon, accentuating the impact of global warming*

acteristic to emerge. That density can be found in an ant colony, which requires a sufficient density of pheromones, or chemicals to bring about social behaviour. Isolated individuals or a population of ants below some threshold do not display any of the attributes of social behaviour that we find in a fully functioning colony. Likewise Amazonian forests need a sufficient density of trees spread across the Basin to generate sufficient cloud forming chemicals to bring about the convection process and downpours of rain that maintain the system further to the west.

The dynamics of the convection process over the Amazon Basin show just how absurd it is to neglect life in helping to determine climatic processes. It defies belief how anyone with a shred of awareness about the Earth we live in, could imagine that climate change is simply a consequence of solar input and the Earth's orbiting of the Sun. A 10°C cooling through cloud formation is no mean feat, when we take into account that since the Earth's origin some 4,500 million years ago, the Sun's luminosity has increased by around one third. Instead of a hotter planet, we have a cooler one, thanks to life in the oceans and on land.

likely temperature increase from a doubling of the pre-industrial concentrations of greenhouse gases.

Typically, those gases collectively known as 'greenhouse gases' — carbon dioxide ($CO_2$), water vapour ($H_2O$), methane ($CH_4$) and nitrous oxide ($N_2O$) — have the potential to resonate with infrared photons, and since each molecular species has its own resonant frequency, all in all they cover a considerable range of the infrared spectrum. Satellites, orbiting above the atmosphere, give us some insight into the extent to which the different gases absorb thermal radiation and at what frequencies. Nonetheless, certain frequencies in the infrared range are unaffected by the presence of greenhouse gases and they pass through the atmosphere without hindrance, taking their heat with them and therefore balancing the Earth's heat budget. The extent to which the atmosphere warms up depends on the concentrations of the different greenhouse gases, at least up to the point of saturation, beyond which the infrared of a particular wavelength passes out to space relatively unhindered.

The year 1957 was a moment of profound significance for global climate studies. It was International Geophysical Year and the United States, then more open to the notion of human-induced climate change, offered to establish an atmospheric laboratory, 4,000 metres up on Mauna Loa, an extinct volcano in Hawaii. It was a perfect site, high up on the mountain, in the middle of the Pacific Ocean and far enough away from large continents and industrial emissions, so as to give time for atmospheric contaminants to mix without prejudicing the results. Charles Keeling, the laboratory's director, had already made a name for himself with his studies of the carbon cycle. His pioneering work gave him the opportunity to identify the degree to which carbon dioxide emissions were rising and from what source, whether fossil fuels, destroyed tropical forests or from other non-fossilized organic material.

Carbon dioxide is the most prevalent of the three, and yet its concentration in terms of overall volume is no more than 380 parts per million, in other words 0.038 percent. Methane comes next with approximately 1.7 parts per million, followed by nitrous oxide with just 0.3 parts per million. Water vapour also acts as a greenhouse gas, but its concentration in the atmosphere depends on the other greenhouse gases to warm the planet's surface air sufficiently such as to cause water to vaporize. In addition, instead of being well mixed in the atmosphere, as are the other gases, water vapour tends to be local to a particular region, its concentration varying from virtually nothing over deserts such as the Atacama in Peru to two percent or more over humid tropical rainforests. For instance, when the trade winds cross the Atlantic and head towards the intertropical convergent zone (ITCZ) over equatorial Brazil, the temperature rises from an average 25°C to 30°C and the saturation vapour pressure increases by more than a third, which results in seven more grammes of vapour being carried in each kilogram of air. In the mid-latitudes a warming of 5°C, from 10°C to 15°C, results in no more than half the change experienced over the tropical Atlantic.

Water vapour therefore gets into the atmosphere on the backs of the other greenhouse gases, yet it is responsible for as much as three quarters of the total heat retained at the Earth's surface. Climatologists, at the time of the Third Climate Change Assessment Report of the IPCC (Intergovernmental Panel on Climate Change) in 2001, predicted that if carbon dioxide concentrations were to double in the atmosphere compared with pre-industrial times, hence from 280 parts per million to 560 parts per million, this would cause global surface temperatures to rise by between 1.2°C and 4.5°C. At the lower temperature, the presence of more water vapour as a result of that warming would amplify the temperature to 1.9°C, hence by more than half again. Presumably at the higher range, the presence of more water vapour would raise the temperatures correspondingly still further.

Without the greenhouse gases, the Earth's surface would be more than 30°C cooler on average. It would be mostly frozen over, with little rain and life would be sparse. Although over time the proportions of greenhouse gases in the atmosphere have varied, being at their lowest during ice ages and increasing with rising temperature, for aeons (1000 million years) they have rarely allowed average surface temperatures to rise or fall to the point when life was threatened. Nonetheless, mass extinctions have occurred, whether because of an asteroid striking the Earth as during the Permian-Triassic age some 185 millions ago when a mountainous mass struck South Africa and left the biggest crater on our planet, or sixty-five million years ago when a smaller but significantly large asteroid struck just off the Yucatan Peninsula in Mexico and precipitated the demise of the dinosaurs, sparing only our feathered friends, the birds. Aside from water vapour, greenhouse gases make up less than one percent of the atmospheric content and, for that reason, seemingly small increments in the concentrations of the greenhouse gases can have a significant impact on surface temperatures.

Which is the chicken, which the egg, lower temperatures leading to a decline in carbon dioxide and methane, or a decline in the

## Global dimming and aircraft

Who would have thought that we might need aircraft vapour trails or something akin to them to produce 'global dimming,' so as to avoid the warming brought about by clearer skies?

Following the grounding of civil aeroplanes in the aftermath of the destruction of the twin towers, surface temperatures rose significantly over the eastern seaboard of the United States, as sunlight made much better contact with the Earth.

Air traffic causes considerable cloudiness, especially when the air is criss-crossed by flight paths, and when condensation-trails form they reflect sunlight back to space. But, unexpectedly, air traffic at night has the exact opposite effect of daytime flights. Apparently, the con-trail build-up during night hours lasts longer because of longer evaporation times, and it seems that during these hours the con-trails, like clouds, hold back the heat at the Earth's surface that under clear night skies would otherwise escape out to space.

We have constantly underestimated the impact of airline traffic. In the late 1960s, in response to a question about the environmental consequences of air traffic, the Federal German government, as it was then, stated that atmospheric pollution from aircraft worldwide would at worst amount to one percent of the total from all sources, including industry and agriculture. Today, air transport produces about one third of the pollution of automobiles, which themselves account for one third of all industrial pollution.

When she was working with the Botanical Institute in Florence, Italy, in the 1990s, Gisela Stief reviewed the impact of air transport on the atmosphere. At that time, at least 10 percent of atmospheric pollutants such as carbon monoxide, unburnt hydrocarbons, nitrogen oxides, sulphur dioxide and dust came from aircraft. Worse, the emissions occurred mostly in the upper troposphere and lower stratosphere, where the impact of contaminants was likely to continue for several years compared to barely one day when emitted from motor vehicles.

The vapour trails of commercial aircraft drastically affect local climate and Stief found a dramatic change in sunlight levels under the flight paths of transcontinental jets as they flew over Italy. In Vallombrosa, in Tuscany, maximum mean summer temperatures fell by 0.6°C compared with forty years ago, while in Siena they were found to have fallen by 0.8°C. Those summer averages hide a precipitous fall of more than 2°C during April and June, in the crucial months of fruit blossoming and ripening. In 1959 Venice received 170.56 watts of sunlight per square metre. By 1987 the amount of sunlight had fallen by one quarter to 131.25 watts per square metre.

*Airplane condensation trails (contrails) across the English Channel [NASA]*

greenhouse gases causing temperatures to fall? In disentangling the timing of ice formation or melt from greenhouse concentrations — evidence obtained from the air trapped in layers of ice in Antarctic and Greenland — Nicholas Shackleton's research group in Cambridge finds that changes in the content of the greenhouse gases anticipate changes in temperature and ice-sheets. That suggests that carbon dioxide is the chicken and it would seem that greenhouse gas concentrations play a primary role in helping determine conditions on the planet and at the very least amplifying them. In essence, since life interacts with the atmosphere, helping to regulate all gases, both gases with no greenhouse properties, such as nitrogen and oxygen, and those with, life clearly must have an impact on climate. Obviously, lower temperatures would take water vapour out of the atmosphere and amplify the decrease in surface temperatures.

Life, through its metabolism, has a daily impact on the amount of carbon dioxide in the atmosphere. Photosynthesis pulls down carbon dioxide, a process which leads to the cellular manufacture of carbohydrates, proteins and all cellular components. Respiration puts it back in the process of transforming carbohydrates to cellular energy in the form of ATP — adenosine tri-phosphate. And, whereas photosynthesis leads to the production of free oxygen, respiration takes it out again. Obviously, if the two opposed activities, respiration and photosynthesis, were in balance, then the overall atmospheric content of the greenhouse gases would barely change from one year to the next. But that is not what is happening.

So strong was life's signal that Charles Keeling's laboratory in Hawaii was able to detect the annual pulse in the uptake of carbon dioxide during the northern hemisphere spring and its release during the autumn and winter months. And measurements showed that that thin skin of life on the Earth's surface was responsible for the movement in and out of the atmosphere of as much as 15 percent of the entire atmosphere's worth of carbon dioxide. Obviously, anything that would diminish the uptake and simultaneously increase the output would rapidly add to the overall greenhouse gas contribution of carbon dioxide. Meanwhile, the local pulse shows a wider oscillation the further north and virtually no signal at the equator. All that is logical given the all-the-year growing conditions at the equator and the highly seasonal conditions near to the Arctic Circle. The southern hemisphere shows a weaker signal all round simply because the continents are grouped in the northern hemisphere while the Pacific Ocean and Southern Atlantic Ocean dominate the south.

Each year, since Keeling's group first started taking measurements of the atmospheric gases in 1958, the concentration of carbon dioxide has been rising steadily in the atmosphere by about 1.5 to 2.0 parts per million, having accelerated in recent years. In 1958, the Earth's atmosphere contained some 316 parts per million (ppm) of carbon dioxide. That had risen to 369 ppm forty years later in 1998 and has now reached approximately 380 ppm. All else being equal, and there being no flush of stored greenhouse gases from soils and permafrost, the concentrations of carbon dioxide are likely to exceed 500 parts per million with sixty years from now, a level higher than at any time over the past forty million years, and all achieved within a century.

## The latest research

Human beings are part of life's spectrum and because of our activities across the face of the Earth, we are unquestionably beginning to affect global climate. The problem is that our predictions of what might happen in the future are full of uncertainties. We do not in truth know for certain whether we have passed critical 'tipping' points or how close we are to them. We do not know the consequences of a sudden change in one part of the system for another and ultimately for ourselves. We have little to go on, apart from the predictions of climate models, but, despite the uncertainties inherent in the models, we must take those predictions seriously, especially now that an increasing number of the major centres for investigating climate are coming to the conclusion that we are in for significant climate change, with all the implications that holds for our being exposed to extreme weather events. Recent findings from the University of Bristol's Department of Earth Sciences, using data from fifty climate change models, seem to leave no doubt that over the next two hundred years, rising temperatures will increase the risk of dangerous climate change, with the threat of increased forest fires, drought and flooding around the world, including Eurasia, eastern China, Canada and the Amazon. Areas of western Africa, southern Europe and eastern US states would be at most risk from diminished water supplies and droughts (BBC report, August 14, 2006). Recent heatwaves throughout Europe may well, it seems, be a taste of things to come.

# 7. Living in Daisyworld?

Have you ever wondered why Christmas trees have the shape they do, coming to a conical point rather than the bushy, straggly tops of most trees? If you guessed that the shape might be perfect for shedding snow, then you may well be right. A pile of snow, weighing heavily down on the branches, will certainly damage them, just as it can roofs after a heavy downfall.

What if there's an additional reason, not necessarily related to the weight of snow, but one that has to do with the tree's evergreen dark-coloured needles? Compared to snow, which reflects light back towards space, the needles absorb light, so warming their environment in the early spring, when the sun barely makes it up over the horizon. That way the pines can get a headstart in their growth and make maximum use of whatever sunlight that is available.

The colour of the Earth, with its different hues and coverings, whether of bare rock, of vegetation, of the deep oceans or of ice, snow and clouds, makes a substantial difference to the planet's energy budget. Were a darker surface to spread out, as when sea-ice in the Arctic Circle melts and vanishes, leaving behind deep blue water, then the Earth retains more heat at its surface and warms up. The warming up melts more ice, exposing more ocean water to the summer sun, thereby adding still more to the warming, so that less ice forms in the winter and there is less to melt next season round.

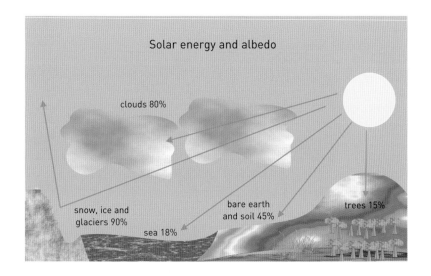

Solar energy and albedo

clouds 80%

snow, ice and glaciers 90%

sea 18%

bare earth and soil 45%

trees 15%

*LEFT:*
*Albedo is the measure of a surface's quality either to reflect light back or to absorb it. Ice or snow reflect sunlight back into the atmosphere, while darker surfaces reflect very little light and so absorb warmth.*

*OPPOSITE:*
*Amadei, Austria  [Sanja Gjenero]*

Such an enhancement is known as a positive feedback in contrast to a self-regulating cycle or negative feedback.

Basically that is what albedo is about; the nature of a surface either to reflect light back or to absorb it. A bright, shining surface, like ice or snow, which reflects light will have an albedo approaching 100 percent, while a black surface, that really gets hot in the sun, has an albedo in the low range. Ice and snow have an albedo in the range of 80 percent, reflecting all but 20 percent back into space, while the ocean's albedo is less than 20 percent, therefore absorbing nigh on 80 percent of all the light that falls over it.

## Lovelock's Daisyworld

Weather is a subset of climate and climate is changing. Climate is changing not just because of the emission of greenhouse gases, but also, as James Lovelock reminds us, life itself has a role in contributing to climate. We have touched on the role of life in weather systems, such as the cloud-forming chemicals emitted everywhere across the vegetative world and not least from phytoplankton in the oceans. We have glanced at the albedo changes, whether light from the Sun is reflected or absorbed, but we have not taken fully into account how far-reaching are the implications of life actually manipulating albedo changes for its own, albeit temporary and opportunistic, ends.

Since life plays such an important part in modifying the atmosphere and thereby altering the surface temperature, James Lovelock wondered whether, in the face of a warming sun, life could actually help regulate surface temperature, to provide optimum conditions overall. A number of renowned biologists had criticized Lovelock's Gaia Theory in which he proposed that life's ability to regulate surface conditions extended to the gases in the atmosphere and to the chemistry of oceans and even rocks. How could life possibly know what conditions were best for it right across the planet? Hadn't life just adapted to the conditions it found, the fittest surviving and leaving their progeny to out-compete rivals for the space offered by the environment?

To show that, in theory, life could adapt its environment to suit itself, rather than simply adapt to given conditions, Lovelock and Andrew Watson, now at the University of East Anglia, devised a simple model of a planet that, like the Earth, orbited a main sequence star which over time got more luminous because of the generation of helium from hydrogen. Their planet, Daisyworld, had two varieties of daisy, one black, the other white, with the planet a neutral colour in between. A planet without daisies would gradually warm from an average surface temperature of around 0°C at the start of the planet's existence, getting hotter and hotter, until 4,500 million years on, the surface temperature would have got up to 40°C.

Lovelock assumed that the optimum temperature for growth would be around 22.5°C, as one finds in real life, and that the daisies would germinate and grow only when the temperature had risen above 5°C, which it would do as the Sun gradually warmed. Black daisies, like the boreal firs versus sedge moss, in germinating, would initially have a considerable advantage over white daisies, by making their immediate environment warmer than it would have been were the planet to have remained lifeless.

Once the temperature approached 20°C the white daisies could begin to come into their own, first sharing the planet on an equal basis with the black daisies, but gradually replacing them as the Sun's luminosity increased, thus keeping the temperature steady at the optimum temperature for growth. When the Sun's luminosity had doubled from the initial state, then not even the high albedo and reflectivity of the white daisies could save them. With their demise the surface temperature of the planet would rapidly reach the temperature that would have been were the planet never blessed with life in the form of daisies.

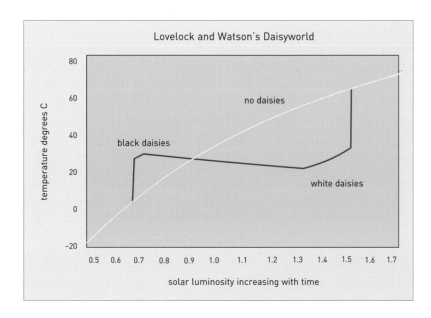

*James Lovelock and Andrew Watson devised a simple computer model of a planet called Daisyworld, where there grow two varieties of daisy, one white, one black. The planet itself is a neutral colour. The graph shows the interplay of temperature on Daisyworld with the predominance of black or white daisies, as the albedo self-regulates in order to provide optimum conditions for the daisies.*

The lesson, using the conifers up north as an example, is that different shades of dark and light will have a profound effect on the heat budget of the planet, either warming it or cooling it. But can we really go along with the Daisyworld mechanism that, as the planet warms, whitish coloured organisms will take over in order to cool their immediate surroundings? The real planet, with its oceans and atmosphere, volcanic activity, and almost chaotic climate, is infinitely more complex.

## Forests and the albedo effect

Albedo plays an essential role in the distribution of the Sun's energy across the planet and has a profound effect on the Earth's heat balance. Richard Betts, at the UK Met Office Hadley Centre for Climate Prediction, showed the importance of considering albedo in elaborating climate models. He was considering the impact of a boreal pine forest spreading northwards as a result of global warming.

In terms of global warming, forestation is considered a bonus, since, with the growth of trees, carbon dioxide is pulled out of the atmosphere, generating biomass and even adding to carbon stores in the soil. The notion is that the take-up of carbon dioxide as a result of photosynthesis therefore offsets some of the emissions of industry and agriculture. But, the supposed uptake of carbon in new growth forests of the boreal region, as a counter to greenhouse gas accumulation in the atmosphere, neglects heat budget changes as a result of the snow-shedding ability of fir trees and their dark needles absorbing the early spring sunshine. When he takes account of albedo changes as a result of tree growth in his models, Betts found somewhat to his astonishment that the greatest impact of the change occurred in Eastern Siberia, where the surface heat absorbed increased by as much as 15 watts per square metre, or equivalent in greenhouse gas emissions of between 90 and 140 tonnes of carbon per hectare.

According to Russian estimates, a newly growing forest will absorb as much as 80 to 120 tonnes of carbon per hectare. Consequently, in the boreal regions the net result of allowing forest to grow and expand its coverage will actually warm up the surface rather than cool it, so helping to melt the permafrost.

Similarly, in Canada the albedo change, equivalent to the emission of 60 to 110 tonnes of carbon per hectare, more than counteracts the average of 60 tonnes of carbon per hectare that would be absorbed by the growing forest. In more temperate regions the gain in emission reductions from newly growing forests will exceed the heat budget from albedo changes because of the paucity of snow. Nonetheless, unless albedo changes are taken into account, the cooling benefits of afforestation and the uptake of carbon may be exaggerated by as much as a factor of 2.

As we have seen, astronomers believe that the sun is now 30 percent more luminous than when the Earth formed. That increase in energy, all else being equal — such as the atmospheric content of greenhouse gases and the planet remaining essentially a watery planet — should have warmed the Earth's surface on average by some 40°C. Yet, the Earth's surface temperature has gone down a few degrees centigrade on average rather than up over the past 100 million years. The absorption of carbon dioxide by terrestrial vegetation and by phytoplankton over this period must have contributed significantly to holding the Earth's temperature down, but albedo changes, in particular the formation of permanent ice-caps at each pole (some eighteen million years ago for Antarctica and some three million years ago for the Arctic), have also played their part, again in a positive feedback process in which a cooler planet is better for plant growth on land and algal growth in the oceans.

## The struggle between dark and light

Without question, the boreal forests stretch their domain northwards as a result of global warming and so benefit themselves from the added warmth they can glean in eliminating the snow from their conical form and basking in the first rays of the Spring Sun. Sphagnum peat moss, on the other hand, releases cloud-forming substances that help blanket it with a cold dense fog that reflects light away and suppresses the growth of trees. A strong tension builds up between the two distinct ecosystems, and whichever wins the contest, tends to take the planet either into an ice age or the more balmy interglacial period. External factors, such as the tilt of the Earth, and where the Earth is and at what time of year, in relation to the Sun, are factors that can initiate a process, which life, through positive feedbacks, then magnifies, so enhancing the switch to a warmer or cooler phase.

Just how and where the sphagnum moss and firs abut against each other makes a profound difference to the local heat budget. No more than a small change and the snowline either advances further south or retreats a little bit further north. When conditions are to the advantage of the sphagnum, we can expect a lowering of temperatures; when

## Bogs and moss

Sphagnum moss not only thrives best in bogs, but actually helps to create its own wet environment by absorbing up to forty times its dry body weight in water. By stimulating anaerobic bacteria (such as the methanogens, Gallionella and Leptothrix) to form a hard pan layer from iron salts in the sediment, the bog iron layer prevents water from draining and provides just the right environment for the sedge moss. Without knowing they had bacteria to thank, the Romans extracted their iron from bogs.

High humidity, despite low winter temperatures, generates the intense mist and fogs that shroud the bog areas. In springtime the light is reflected away and the moss, which can out-compete pines under those cold, humid, even acid conditions, keeps the boreal forests at bay. It is even plausible that an extensive cover of sphagnum moss spreading out over the northern (boreal) region helps accelerate the Earth slipping back into an ice age, while the spread of boreal forests, as we are seeing now, has the opposite effect and accelerates warming.

*Bog in Poland  [Griszka Niewiadomsk]*

they are to the advantage of the conifers, then we can expect a warming, simply because of changes in albedo.

In northern Canada, in the district of Keewatin, snowbanks may not melt away until the end of July. Less than a month later the first snows may arrive. Were the summer to shorten by just three weeks, suggests Reid Bryson, the US climatologist from the University of Wisconsin-Madison, then new snow would pile on old and a new round of glaciation could be in the making.

For several million years, ice ages have dominated the state of the planet, lasting one hundred thousand years or so, with relatively short breaks when the Earth basks in an interglacial period, just as we are experiencing now. The emergence from the last ice some fourteen thousand years ago undoubtedly had a lot to do with creating the right, stable conditions for the development of agriculture, hence a sedentary life and an explosion in the human population. The Earth's orbit, whether more circular or elliptical, the angle of tilt and whether, like a top spinning, the line of tilt takes the North Pole to the east or west of centre, all play their part in taking the planet in and out of ice ages. But, if such cycles in the trajectory of the Earth around the Sun marginally alter the amount of energy bathing the planet, life in part through changing albedo, is the factor that accentuates such 'external forcing' factors.

In that respect, the spreading southwards of the great peat bogs of the tundra, whether in Canada or Siberia, by dint of generating mists and low-lying clouds, cool the boreal region by as much as 3°C. The snow that falls through such cooling adds its own high albedo, and tends to stay on the ground for an additional eighteen days. That fact alone is enough to send the ice creeping southwards, gradually covering the landscape, until in places it reaches several thousand metres thick.

But, as explained so beautifully by Stephan Harding in his book *Animate Earth,* the jostling tension between the forest and ice may well have another edge to it. The actual boundary layer between the cold air travelling southwards from the Arctic Circle and the warm air coming up from the tropics in the south is where the tundra and the forest meet, rather like the fine thread of green, abutting against the desert, as seen from Herod's fort in Judea. Is that interface, that wrestle between tundra and forest, simply a result of a superimposed climate, or does the vegetation play its part in determining whether that line shifts more northwards or southwards?

For one, the low albedo of the forest, or alternatively the high albedo of the tundra, plays back into the climate processes that

*Teklanika River, Denali National Park, Alaska. A gray wolf hunting a bull moose. Could interactions between prey and predator affect when the world plunges in and out of ice ages?*
[Eastcott Momatiuk, Getty Images]

generate the polar and tropical air currents. Where those currents meet — the cold front — is where the snow falls, as the warm, more humid air flow is forced upwards by the denser, colder, drier air from the north, and where the snow falls that is where the tundra best grows.

Harding takes the story still further, almost into the realms of fantasy, but still nested within a new understanding as to the relationship between life on this planet and climate. He asks whether the hunting behaviour of wolves and their relationship to moose would affect climate by having an impact on that almost magical line between tundra and forest. The story goes a little like this: when the snow is thick on the ground, moose find the going rough and the wolves group themselves into larger packs in order to optimize their hunting strategy. That takes the moose population down, to the advantage of the boreal forest, because its saplings will have a better chance of taking hold. More mature trees then follow and the zone of warming through albedo changes becomes more extensive.

All that feeds back into the natural climate system and causes less snow to fall in the southernmost parts of the interface between the two distinct ecosystem types, the sedge moss tundra and the boreal conifers. The moose population, at least in that relatively snowless region, obtains greater mobility and more easily evades being hunted down by wolves, which themselves are now having to hunt in smaller groups, to maximize their chances. More moose means more saplings are eaten and the more easily the sedge moss can penetrate further south, so essentially taking the climate interface line down with them.

As Harding admits, it will be difficult and controversial to prove that such subtle changes in hunting behaviour could play back on the climate. But, the point is made, how feedbacks in the larger system essentially take their cue from what is happening in the local, where organisms and species jostle for survival, in a dance of interdependency.

The overarching theme in such an enchanting explanation is the distribution of energy in the climate system, just as we have seen from the Amazonian example where the humid rainforest plays a critical role in that energy distribution. Again, changes in albedo play their part, the tropical rainforest, like sedge moss, cooling its environment by forming clouds and converting water to vapour, with all the energy that such a phase change requires.

Clearly our planet is made up of a myriad of such stories where life acts out its particular relationship to its local environment and consequently to the larger system that is climate. Given the extraordinary complexity of life's interactions, it is hardly surprising that climatologists have largely failed to include such processes or even the possibility of such processes in their models. But attitudes are changing.

A little over a decade ago, in the second of its Assessment Reports (1995), the Intergovernmental Panel on Climate Change (IPCC) stated somewhat categorically that life's interaction with climate was of secondary importance in the factors leading to climate change and therefore unlikely to change significantly the conclusions reached by climatologists in projecting the results of their models. That pragmatic approach underwent something of a sea change by the time of the Third Assessment Report a few years later in 2001, as the result of pioneer work by climatologists at the UK Met Office's Hadley Centre. Instead of leaving life's activities, including carbon uptake from the atmosphere, in a static box, climatologists at the Centre, such as Peter Cox and Richard Betts, incorporated a dynamic vegetative cycle into the circulation models, such that life would alter its relationship to the atmosphere and its greenhouse gases depending on changes in climate. The Hadley Centre, therefore, accepted the notion that life would have its own feedbacks on the climate system,

## Using the albedo principle in building

We all know that dark rocks exposed to the Sun of mid-summer get uncomfortably hot compared to a white-washed surface. So, why not use that feature to warm houses or even cool them? The French inventor Felix Trombe did just that in developing housing: he exploited the albedo effect of dark surfaces so as to use sunshine hours to provide a steady supply of heat to the interior of a building.

The Trombe wall, facing southwards, is a thick concrete wall coated on the outside with blackened foil and shielded with a double glazing of glass that stands a few inches away from the wall. Light enters as in a greenhouse, and just as in a greenhouse holds the heat back so that the infrared has time to penetrate into the wall and across into the house itself, warming up the interior. Experiments with walls that contain special salts that melt in the heat and then give up the heat on crystallizing as the temperature declines, can increase a wall's capacity for absorbing and then delivering heat by a factor of 400.

More elaborate versions have ducts leading from the warmed surface to the house interior, thereby circulating warm air. And the sun can also be used to cool the house by opening a vent in the Trombe wall so that hot air escapes and draws in air from the interior of the house. If that same air has passed over a large bowl of water, the water in evaporating will keep the house cool. Until modern times, houses in Egypt used a comparable way of cooling the house interior. They had a south-facing open court-yard and a north facing one which had vegetation growing in it. Vents throughout the house enabled a current of air to flow from the north courtyard to the south, the air being passed over semi-porous 'mazara' jars filled with Nile water. That system was as effective as an array of air conditioners. Furthermore, on a cool, sunless day the current of air would diminish or stop all together — none other than a self-governing cooling system.

Living at 12,000 feet in the Himalayan plateau above the tree line, and getting their water from melting glaciers and snow, Ladakhis have traditionally burnt the dung from their yaks and dzhos, a mixed-breed animal between a yak and a cow, to warm their stone houses when the outside winter temperature has fallen, perhaps to as low as −40 °C. That has the disadvantage of burning a valuable fertilizer and of generating eye-damaging smoke.

Helena Norberg-Hodge first visited Ladakh more than thirty years ago, when India opened its borders up to the West. She was struck then by the self-sufficiency and lack of 'need' within Ladakhi society.

But that all began to change when the Indian Government built a paved road to the region, so opening up the country to outside interests. Paraffin oil could now be brought in from India and Ladakhis were rapidly becoming dependent on it for heating their houses. They now had to pay for their energy instead of deriving it locally. But Ladakh endures intense sun throughout the year and Helena therefore saw it would be the ideal place to use the Trombe wall. Over the years she has managed to persuade Ladakhis that they could get all the heat they required without burning oil, simply by painting one wall of their house black and covering it with glass, while allowing an insulating layer of air between. That way the interior warms up even in the bitter cold of the Ladakh winter and saves on burning animal manure or on buying expensive kerosene.

*Thiksey, India. Ladakhi Buddhist monks stand in a doorway.*
*[AFP/Getty Images]*

by changing the Earth's albedo, for example, and by adding or subtracting to the concentrations of greenhouse gases in the atmosphere. They were among the first models to indicate the possibility that soils, having been carbon 'sinks' for millennia could switch almost overnight to becoming 'sources,' thereby releasing vast quantities of greenhouse gases into the atmosphere.

In taking such integrated models into account, the IPCC began to change its tune, nevertheless admitting the 'extreme' difficulty of detecting climate-induced changes in most ecological and social systems. In the words of the 2001 report:

> this is because of the complexity of these systems, their many non-linear feedbacks, and their sensitivity to a large number of climatic and non-climatic factors, all of which are expected to change simultaneously ... As future climate extends beyond the boundaries of all empirical knowledge ... it becomes more likely that actual outcomes will include surprises and unanticipated rapid changes.

## Life on Earth and cloud-forming

Forests, particularly tropical forests, as well as certain kinds of phytoplankton in the ocean, can help generate planet-cooling clouds through releasing volatile organic compounds such as isoprenes that act as cloud condensation nuclei, rather like seeding a liquid with an impurity that hastens its crystallization. The clouds, like snow and ice, reflect light back into space, and so have an albedo that is considerably higher than that of the vegetation at the Earth's surface.

In 1971 James Lovelock travelled to the South Atlantic in the research vessel Shackleton. He was using his electron capture device, an invention that in one stroke had brought about a millionfold improvement in the detection of trace quantities of gases in the atmosphere. Lovelock was the first to detect chlorofluorocarbons in the lower atmosphere, so awakening some scientists to the possibility that, by rising into the stratosphere, the CFCs could destroy the ozone layer and leave us open to damaging ultraviolet B. Later, through having revealed the chemistry of ozone destruction, two of the scientists concerned, Mario Molina and Rowland Sherwood, received the Nobel Prize.

During his travels down towards Antarctica, Lovelock detected trace quantities of DMS — dimethyl-sulphide — a volatile compound that is swiftly oxidized to sulphur dioxide. The sulphuric acid particles that form from this process act as cloud condensation nuclei, resulting in marine stratus clouds that, apart from bearing rain, form a light-reflecting layer which cools the ocean surface. The same clouds transport the sulphur to the continents, providing terrestrial life with an essential nutrient.

Where does the DMS come from? As Lovelock points out, it is emitted from minute, one-celled phytoplankton called coccolithophores. These plankton, with their exquisite calcareous shells, form enormous milky white blooms stretching for hundreds of miles and, while growing, produce an organic sulphur compound which prevents their drying out in salty waters. The sulphur compound is therefore known as an osmolyte. However, on the death of the organism, the osmolyte breaks down to DMS.

What possible advantage can the attribute of cloud-forming be to the coccolithophore? One suggestion is that by altering the albedo, the clouds bring about cold spots in the surface waters that cause local currents which bring up nutrients from below, thereby feeding the phytoplankton. That being so, the bloom benefits as a result of the death of the individual. Another idea is that the up-draughts of air brought about by the differential cooling of the ocean surface from the cloud-formation will draw up micro-organisms such as the coccolithophores and cast them down again, perhaps hundreds of miles away, when the clouds release their water vapour as rain.

Irrespective of any advantage to the coccolithophores, the clouds help to cool the planet, and they bear rain and nutrients such as sulphur. It is surely no coincidence that coccolithophores evolved at the time that life was beginning to invade the land. The Earth's albedo is therefore a constantly changing attribute which depends largely on life's ability, through its growth and evolution, to bring about substantial changes to the planet's heat budget. Changes in water from light-absorbing liquid to light-reflecting clouds, ice and snow, contribute the most as to how much heat remains at the Earth's surface. In all its phases, water is responsible for 94 percent of the Earth's albedo and a little swing here and there will make a profound difference to the Earth warming or cooling. Furthermore, a shift one way will lead to positive feedback and an acceleration of the effect until a new climate disturbance swings the trend back the other way. In fact, albedo, in combination with the uptake or release of greenhouse gases, is perhaps the most critical factor in holding the Earth's temperature relatively steady, as shown by Lovelock's *Daisyworld*.

*Coccolithophore blooming in the English Channel, June 2001  [NASA]*

*Climate scientists marching towards the abyss?*
[*Richard Wilson,* The Doomsday Funbook]

# 8. Fiddling While the Planet Burns

## *The politics of climate change*

In March 2005, the UK government sponsored a major climate conference at the Meteorological Office in Exeter. There, a number of scientists, including some from the prestigious Met Office Hadley Centre for Climate Prediction, maintained that we have practically reached the limits (400 parts per million by volume) of $CO_2$ in the atmosphere beyond which dramatic and unpredictable changes will take place. Somewhat out of step with such dire predictions, Sir David King, government chief scientific adviser, stressed that we could get to 550ppm — essentially a doubling of pre-industrial

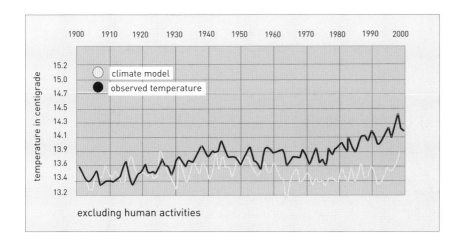

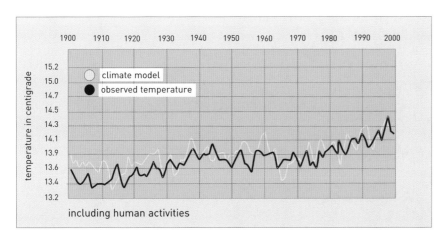

*LEFT (TOP & BOTTOM): Historic climate models which do not take human activities into account (top) show a high discrepancy with the actual temperatures observed over the last hundred years. Models which include human activities as a factor (bottom) show a close correspondence with recorded temperature patterns.*

levels — with acceptable climatic disruption. Perhaps he had been pressured by the government to make it appear that we had more time before disaster struck, so giving some credence to current government policies on greenhouse gas reductions.

We don't really know the critical tipping point concentrations of $CO_2$ in the atmosphere. Our dilemma is that action may be over-reaction, presumably at some cost to the 'economy' — and doubly expensive in terms of trade were we in Britain to go it alone — but on the other hand, we could somewhat complacently continue polluting only then to discover we have passed the limits.

The very idea of tipping points suggests that present trends may not necessarily signal the future. Oceans may have absorbed carbon dioxide in the past, only to begin releasing all that has been recently absorbed. A warmer ocean, apart from expanding because of the extra warmth, can contain less carbon dioxide in its surface waters than a cooler one, but that has to be measured against rates of absorption increasing because of higher carbon dioxide concentrations in the atmosphere and therefore a higher 'partial pressure' of the gas. And if the oceans do absorb more carbon dioxide that will lead to greater acidification of the surface layers. A more acid ocean is one which has a harmful effect on organisms such as corals and phytoplankton because their calcareous shells literally dissolve away, so bringing about their death. And since phytoplankton enhance the ocean uptake of carbon dioxide as a result of photosynthesis, we can see how delicate is the balance between uptake and excessive acidification. To add to our concerns, a warmer ocean forms stable, capping layers of warm water that prevent the chemically rich deeper waters breaking through to the surface and so providing the photosynthesizing plankton with essential nutrients. The limits to the growth of plankton, their death from acidification, plus warmer surface waters, could lead to releases of $CO_2$ which would double atmospheric concentrations in a matter of years.

Worrying indeed, the latest Met Office Hadley Centre models show significantly more heating over the coming century compared with earlier models simply as a result of taking into account the dynamics of the carbon cycle. Indeed, in response to warming temperatures, soils and the biomass they support may switch from storing carbon dioxide in the form of organic compounds into burning them up. What, in effect, would be the consequence were plant and soil respiration to gain the upper hand over photosynthesis? Carbon dioxide levels in the atmosphere could rise by another third from that source alone.

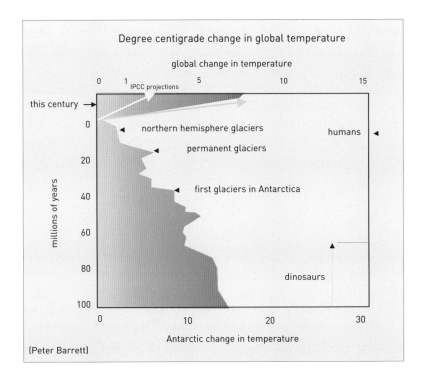

(Peter Barrett)

*Within one century, our greenhouse gas emissions could lead to surface temperatures on Earth that have not been experienced for one hundred million years*

And what about methane, now leaking from Siberia, as a result of permafrost melting? When we take all such factors into account we could find ourselves facing a four-fold increase in atmospheric greenhouse gases during the current century compared with pre-industrial times, up to 1000ppm, and temperatures over the land surface rising far more than currently predicted, using those out-dated models that do not include a dynamic vegetative carbon cycle. Such temperatures have not been experienced on Earth for more than 100 million years, when no permanent ice-caps existed, when the sea-level was many metres higher than today, when dinosaurs roamed and human beings were barely a mote in the eye of evolution.

As human beings we believe in trends, in small accumulative changes that can be reversed if only we were to take a step back. The politics of climate change are based on such a notion. In that respect, the Kyoto Protocol, to which governments agreed in 1997, and which has since been ratified by 186 countries, demands that Annexe 1 industrialized countries collectively reduce their greenhouse gas emissions 5.2 percent by the deadline date of 2012. Some countries, such as Britain, have offered and signed up to doing more, others in Europe, such as Spain, somewhat less, but it is as if meeting the target we can sigh with relief that we have constrained climate change to manageable proportions.

In fact, with our very survival at stake, we must consider the Kyoto Protocol as nothing more than a first faltering step in bringing nations together in agreement that action has to be taken. We will have to take far more serious action once the second commitment period of the Protocol follows on from 2012, or the worst prognoses of the impact of climate change may prove all too real.

But our current obsession with greenhouse gas emissions, and the resolve of those countries which have signed up to the Kyoto Protocol (see below) to start curbing such emissions, is only part of the story. If, magically, we were able, virtually overnight, to stop burning fossil fuels and could bring global greenhouse emissions down by 80 percent, and so avoid further global warming, but still we ravaged the planet of its natural resources, ripping out forests, constructing mega-cities, pouring cement in great swathes across the countryside to transport millions upon millions of vehicles, we would still face the potential for dramatic climate change.

Tropical forests, for example, play a big role in climate by converting the energy from the sun into water vapour that then fuels clouds and so helps cool the Earth. Water vapour embodies energy in the form of the latent heat of evaporation and the equivalent amount of energy required to form water vapour from liquid water gets released when the vapour condenses. The air masses from the tropics, carrying water vapour with them, are therefore energy conductors, distributing rain and energy simultaneously to regions outside the tropics. Tropical forests play a vital role in maintaining the hydrological cycle such that water gets from the oceans to the continents and back again in the rivers. Nothing can be a more dramatic example of this process than the River Amazon, which has nearly one quarter of the flow of all the world's rivers combined.

When we destroy such forests, in one stroke we prevent the absorption of greenhouse gases while simultaneously releasing the carbon that has been stored over centuries, if not millennia. Were all the remaining Amazon forests to be lost in the Brazilian part of the Basin, then the potential net committed emissions would amount to as much as 77 GtC. That amount, Philip Fearnside of the Institute for Amazon Research points out, would be 10 percent higher than the 70 GtC that could be gained from full implementation of the Kyoto Protocol (including the United States and Australia) together with a 1 percent compounded reduction per year in the emissions of the Annexe B countries (developed) from fossil fuel burning between 2010 and 2100.

## The rainforest and carbon gases

The healthy forest accumulates carbon from the atmosphere in the form or organic material and biomass. According to John Grace, of Edinburgh University and others, who have been contributing to the Large-scale Biosphere-Atmosphere Programme (LBA) in Brazil, the average uptake of carbon dioxide over the Amazon Basin in non El Niño years may be as much as 0.56 GtC per year (109 tonnes of carbon per year), hence equivalent to 8 percent of total annual emissions from all human activities. Just on their carbon uptake alone, says Grace, such rainforests are providing an irreplaceable global environment service.

The downside is the release of carbon from deforestation. Philip Fearnside of Brazil's Amazon Research Institute in Manaus estimates such carbon emissions as 'net committed emissions,' which take account both of decay following a fire and of any future reabsorption of carbon by the new landscape. During the 1980s the average annual net committed emissions from land-use change in Brazil was 0.556 billion tonnes of carbon; hence about one-eleventh the 6.4 GtC (gigatonnes of carbon) emissions from fossil fuel burning across the planet and just under one-quarter of the total 2.4 GtC emissions from the tropics. Indeed, deforestation in the Brazilian Amazon makes per capita emissions of carbon as bad as any Briton's.

Unverified statements that whatever vegetation replaces the forest, such as pasture, it will, over time, regain all the carbon that has been lost, have proved little but wishful thinking: field research indicates that 7 percent at most of the original carbon gets reabsorbed over time by the replacement landscape. Another mistake is to ignore the carbon release from the decomposition and decay of the remaining biomass after the initial burn. According to Philip Fearnside, the final tally of carbon emitted from burning felled trees is likely to be at least three times greater than measured at the time of the fire. As a result, the emissions in any one year may be augmented by emissions from deforestation that took place in a previous year.

## The Kyoto Protocol

In 1988, as a result of growing concern that human activities might be influencing climate in ways that could be deleterious, especially to global agriculture, the United Nations Environment Programme (UNEP), together with the World Meteorological Organization (WMO), established an Intergovernmental Panel on Climate Change. The intention was that scientists concerned with climate could get together and form a consensus as to the likely future of climate over the next hundred years or so.

At the Rio Conference on the Human Environment in 1992 the delegates agreed to the setting up of the Framework Convention on Climate Change (UNFCCC) the task of which was to forge an agreement between nations as to the best ways to combat climate change. The IPCC was the vehicle by which the UNFCCC could request action from the global community, and that resulted in the Kyoto Protocol.

The Protocol came into being as a result of a Conference of the Parties (COPs) meeting in Japan in December 1997, the whole process being held in the balance until the United States, then the world's biggest emitter of greenhouse gases, agreed to sign up. Two years later, at the COP meeting in Buenos Aires in 1999, the participating countries decided, after much deliberation, that the developed countries, when lumped together and including the United States, Australia and Japan, should commit themselves to a reduction of 5.2 percent in their greenhouse gas emissions, compared to an inventory of such emissions taken in each country for a 1990 baseline. Participating countries had to comply by 2012 at the latest.

But the Protocol could become obligatory only when sufficient industrialized countries, encompassing 55 percent of the global total of human-induced emissions, had ratified. Then the blow came, four years after the Protocol's birth: the United States and Australia reneged and it looked extremely chancy that the Kyoto Protocol could survive, at least long enough to be become obligatory to its signatories. Russia was the key. It had one thing going for signing up; because of the serious downturn in its economy after the baseline year of 1990, plus the shutting down of old, inefficient, coal-burning factories and power stations, it had carbon credits to hand, or as Greenpeace, Friends of the Earth and other critics would put it, 'hot air,' when compared to the emissions of 1990 and further back. Therefore, upon ratification, it could legally engage in carbon trading, getting carbon credits simply by selling off the short fall between its actual and permitted emissions. On the other hand, hanging on to its carbon credits would, said Russian economists, restrict its economy, even though Russia would have had the opportunity to replace obsolete, inefficient and polluting industrial plants with state of the art modern ones.

Despite pressure from the United States not to ratify and pressure from the European Union to do so, Russia, with its 17 percent of world emissions, finally ratified in 2005, thereby pushing the total of committed countries to above the necessary 55 percent. Ninety days later, the treaty came properly into force, by which all the signatories had to commit themselves to reducing emissions of six key greenhouse gases to an average of 5.2 percent below 1990 levels by 2012. Countries which failed to meet the targets would face penalties and the prospect of having to make deeper cuts in future.

While backing the pact was more a political move than an environmental one for Russia, with President Putin agreeing to fast-track the ratification of Kyoto in September 2004, only because of the European Union's promise to support Russia in its bid to join the World Trade Organization, it did get over the hurdle of sufficient overall support. In addition, it did show the United States, as well as Australia, that they were out of line with world opinion and concerns about climate change and its consequences.

An essential part of the treaty, the notion and practice of carbon trading received an enormous boost. UNEP — the United Nations Environment Programme — predicted that as much as two million million US dollars would be traded by the end of the first compliance period in 2012. On the other hand, the rules are clear in that countries which fail to meet their targets will have to pay a 30 percent penalty for the shortfall in their agreed reductions, will be barred from carbon trading and will be forced to take corrective measures to catch up.

In terms of impact on global emissions of greenhouse gases, the protocol will make little or negligible difference, because the world's two biggest emitters, the US and China, are unlikely to reduce their outputs or at least get them below 1990 levels. China, although a ratifying country, does not yet have to reduce its emissions. In effect, it is hardly surprising that the United States did not sign up, since by the time the first commitment period will have reached its final date in 2012, the United States is likely to be 30 percent or more up on its emissions of 1990. And if only it had been better news from the rest of the industrialized countries; it seems that hardly one of those that ratified will meet its targets.

Without the United States on board, nor indeed Australia — the two countries combined accounting for 32 percent of global emissions — how much impact will Kyoto have? The IPCC estimated in 1998, at the Conference of Parties' meeting in Buenos Aires, that the 5.2 percent reduction across the board of industrialized countries including the USA and Australia, would reduce global temperatures by no more than 0.1°C as against the minimum 1.5°C rise expected over the next fifty years.

That slight potential drop in predicted temperature is barely enough to make a jot of difference, but nevertheless, for those nations that signed up, it demonstrates a conviction that humans are a cause of climate change and global warming, and is simultaneously a commitment to preventing further change. But, few would deny that it is too little too late and critics of the Kyoto Protocol, who nonetheless may be in favour of action, point out that much more stringent emission reductions will be needed, 60 percent or greater, within decades, to avert the impacts of serious climate change. The reality is that total global emissions are likely to rise at least by 10 percent compared to the 1990 baseline year, and as the years pass the further away we are from meeting the minimal targets of the Protocol.

Do countries plan to negotiate further emission reductions? Kyoto requires that parties to the Protocol begin negotiating in 2005, toward a second round of commitments, yet it is unlikely that ratifying countries will agree to more stringent targets post-2012 unless the United States participates. In resisting commitment to the Protocol, the United States does have a valid gripe — although its reaction is dangerously short-sighted — in its complaint that developing countries with rapidly increasing emissions, such as India and China, have, for the time being, been left off the hook, so giving their rapidly expanding exports a distinct advantage, especially when combined with cheap labour.

One possibility is that the new round of talks will focus more broadly on ways to modify Kyoto or structure a successor agreement acceptable to all the major emitting countries. One large lacuna in Kyoto Protocol One was the exclusion of existing tropical forests within the scope of carbon trading, while new plantations on degraded lands were made part of the deal through the Clean Development Mechanism (CDM), by which a donor industrialized signed-up country could, as a result of its investment in such a project, benefit from the supposed carbon pulled out the atmosphere by the growing trees. A dubious project if there ever as one, especially when we take account of the substantial emissions of greenhouse gases from the destruction of existing tropical rainforests.

One cogent critic of Kyoto is Dr Hermann Scheer, Member of the German Parliament (Bundestag), President of the European Association for Renewable Energies EUROSOLAR and General Chairman of the World Council for Renewable Energy (WCRE). In a recent letter to the *Intelligence Unit,* an international organization that uses emails for well-known politicians and political commentators to air different views, Scheer stated that, because of the conference process, governments have a perfect excuse to postpone any environmental overhaul of their respective domestic energy sectors

*Greenpeace activists in Hamburg, Germany, erected a four metre tall replica of the Statue of Liberty in the Alster estuary on October 22, 2004, as a protest against the US government's refusal to sign the Kyoto Protocol on reducing global greenhouse gas emissions. Russia's President Putin approved the Kyoto agreement in September 2004. It was ratified by the Russian Parliament, the Duma, in May 2005.*
[*Patrick Lux, PAP*]

## The rainforests: Kyoto misses the point

A major problem with the Kyoto Protocol is that while Article 2 establishes that developed countries should 'protect and enhance sinks and reserves, promote sustainable forest management practices, afforestation and reforestation,' Article 12 ensures that existing forests are not included. The Protocol therefore reflects the wishes of environmentalists, and in particular those of western Europe and the United States, who have been strongly opposed to the notion that 'Clean Development Mechanisms' (CDMs) include avoided deforestation on the understandable grounds that the carbon is already contained in the forest and soil.

Such environmentalists were justifiably worried that industrialized countries such as the US would wriggle out of their responsibilities to cut greenhouse gas emissions through claims that the existence and expansion of natural forests within state boundaries were doing the job for them. Hence, the environmentalists have argued that if avoided deforestation were to be legitimized in the CDMs, those countries (and companies) benefiting from any carbon trading on forest conservation would need to do little more than look around for the cheapest carbon offsets and count those against their own emissions. To date the Brazilian government has expressed its opposition to the inclusion of forest conservation and its corollary, a reduction in the rate of deforestation, as being legitimate opportunities for CDMs. Clearly the Brazilian government has believed that it will gain more through inviting in external investment in exploiting the land beneath the forests than it ever would through gaining carbon credits. That view is valid only if the true ecological and climatological services of the Amazon Basin are ignored.

on the basis that they can do little or nothing until a global treaty has been agreed and ratified by all and sundry, including the USA.

The effect of the climate change negotiations, Scheer remarks, has been to preserve the *status quo*, while giving ample room to the energy industry to lobby governments. The process has been helped along as a result of market liberalization, a process which has received hefty governmental and legislative backing. Scheer is particularly concerned that:

> ... movement towards sustainable energy supplies is conspicuous by its absence, and that the power of those primarily responsible for global warming is structurally more entrenched than ever.
> It comes as no surprise that the most important topics are not even up for discussion: not global carbon dioxide taxation, nor an end to the tax exemption for aviation fuel (although the rapid growth in air travel represents the greatest single danger to the climate), nor the abolition of conventional energy subsidies, currently amounting to USD 300,000 million a year.

## The rhetoric and the reality

The United Kingdom, first under Margaret Thatcher's premiership and then under Tony Blair's vociferously expressed the need to tackle global warming. Blair offered to go beyond the demands of the Kyoto Protocol, which requested the UK to make cuts of up to 10 percent by 2012. Instead Blair suggested ambitiously that the UK could get closer to 20 percent.

The UK, post-1990, had already reduced its emissions by as much as 7 percent compared to the baseline year, but that was largely because of Margaret Thatcher's success in deregulating the electricity supply industry. As a result, Britain's newly privatized utilities moved rapidly away from coal, burning cheaper natural gas instead, which, for each unit of electricity generated, produced 25 percent less carbon emissions than did coal. But, the reality is that the UK is falling short by a considerable margin as energy use, particularly of fossil fuels, continues to rise. Recent figures, supplied by the Department of Trade and Industry, show that carbon dioxide emissions from the UK have been rising, therefore eating into the gains made from switching fuels in the electricity sector. Emissions rose by 2.2 percent in 2003 and 1.5 percent in 2004 and currently are no more than 4 percent below 1990 levels.

The reality is that recent energy demand in the UK is growing at almost double the rate of the past half century, the Department of Trade and Industry (DTI) predicting that the current per annum increase of 0.9 percent will continue at least until 2010. Energy demand is up in all sectors of the UK economy — in transport, electricity and space heating. The DTI predicts that the UK's total emissions will decrease from 159.6m to 141.9m tonnes (carbon) between 1990 and 2010 — down by 11 percent — but then increase again to 144.8m tonnes by 2020. In essence, over the three decades from 1990, emissions from power stations are forecast to go down by 36 percent, and those from industry by 14 percent, but from road traffic to rise by 35 percent. To curb emissions from transport is therefore a major challenge.

In fact, when Tony Blair chaired the G-10 meeting at Gleneagles in 2005, the expectation was that he would be unyielding with regard to Britain's commitment to Kyoto. But he caved in to the United States, and their adherence to the notion that reductions are better left to market forces, including carbon trading. What is true in the UK, at least in overall terms, is true elsewhere in the industrialized countries, although some such as Sweden and Iceland, are determined to have fossil fuel free economies in the next few decades, and all that without nuclear power.

## Rising temperatures

While the bickering and bargaining goes on, climate change is accelerating. Sir David King, the UK Government's Chief Scientist, has warned that the Earth is likely to experience a temperature rise of at least 3°C, on account of world governments failing to agree on reducing emissions of greenhouse gases. Sea-levels would rise dramatically, leaving large sections of the world's coastlines under water, while worldwide, delicately-balanced ecosystems would collapse and four hundred million people would go hungry. Computer modelling, said King, showed that by the end of this century, carbon dioxide levels would be more than 500 parts per million (ppm) — double those of the Industrial Revolution. The impact would include a loss of up to 400 million tonnes of cereal production, and put between 1.2 thousand million and three thousand million people — half the world's current population — at risk of water shortages.

A fifth of coastal wetlands would be lost and half of nature reserves damaged, 'yet we are saying 500ppm in the atmosphere is probably the best we can achieve through global agreement.'

In their report, *Avoiding Dangerous Climate Change,* the UK Met Office's Hadley Centre, modelled the likely effects of a 3°C rise, hinging on stabilizing carbon dioxide at a level of 550 parts per million in the atmosphere. To allow us to get to that level of concentrations in the atmosphere was a mighty risk, said King. That figure is almost double the pre-industrial level of two centuries ago, yet, according to Tony Blair's advisors, the lowest figure achievable worldwide, as developing countries continued to increase their emissions, and the US refused to cut its $CO_2$.

The Institute for Public Policy Research (IPPR) has criticized Professor King for accepting global temperatures could rise above 2°C. And Friends of the Earth director, Tony Juniper, has said: 'It is technologically possible to reduce significantly our emissions and deliver 2°C. Professor King should be pressing for government policies to deliver on this rather than accepting the current lack of political will and talking of 3°C as an inevitability.' Meanwhile, the US administration has been unwilling to contemplate a $CO_2$ threshold. President Bush's chief climate adviser, James Connaughton, pronounced that he did not believe anyone could forecast a safe level and cutting greenhouse gas emissions could harm the world economy. In the face of such an attitude from Washington, several states on the east coast, and now California too — with state governor Arnold Schwarzenegger's recent announcement of a new stringent policy on pollution — have introduced their own curbs on emissions.

The problem is that such new legislation takes effect slowly and over years. Climate change and global warming are not going to hang around while the world gets its act together, and we now face the disturbing situation that we may already have tumbled over the edge of a number of climatic tipping points and, like Humpty Dumpty, be unable to get back in one piece on the wall. In fact, the consensus deliberations of the scientists informing the process are all very well, but like a classroom that panders to the average and poor student, climatologists, who developed models predicting more rapid and devastating climate change, have seen their conclusions marginalized and watered down, so as to meet the requirements of the lowest common denominator of credibility.

# 9. Our Future on This Planet

It is the nature of climate to change. Conditions are never the same. The sun is more luminous, more energetic, as time goes on, quite aside from sunspots and the sun's own varying cycle of rhythms. The Earth's orbit and how it is affected by the conjunction of the other planets and masses in our solar system, let alone through gravitational and other cosmic forces across space, also displays its own varying cycle of rhythms that help push the modern earth in and out of ice ages. In addition the earth has its own peculiar characteristics, such as its atmosphere of life-regulated greenhouse gases or its varying colours that like a chameleon's skin, flicker through a range of light-absorbing or light-reflecting colours, as the seasons change. And now the earth has human beings who impose their own conditions upon the earth, contradicting the activities of life support systems by ripping them out and replacing them with less than adequate substitutes.

Ignorance may have been bliss, until now. But, with modern communications, we are all linked, whether we like it or not, to what is happening elsewhere in the world. An indigenous person in the Putumayo tropical rainforest now has the ability, through television or radio, to know that the Inuit in the Arctic Circle are facing a world that is turning into melted mush; he or she will also know that the seasons are changing, that when it used to rain it is now scorchingly dry, that the palm trees by the swamp, so important in the subsistence of the Siona or Kofan peoples in the Colombian Amazon, so important too for threatened species of woolly monkey, are no longer giving fruit and, vice versa, that the rains when they do come are damaging in their sheer intensity and then they are gone. We all know, whoever we are, whatever we do, that climate is changing dramatically and many of us are worried, not least the majority of climatologists and meteorologists who try to make sense of a tricky and chaotic system that, nonetheless, follows rather than defies the laws of physics.

Since our own responsibility in bringing about climate change is no longer in doubt, what can we do? Are we already too late? Have we already exceeded certain limits and passed those tipping points when the entire climate system jumps to a different state that may be less than hospitable to the majority of human beings? And we should remember that other great and elaborate civilizations, like those of the Maya in Guatemala, the Zenues in northern Colombia, or the Sumerians of Mesopotamia, came to grief in good measure because of a sudden flip in climate, no more than a brief spell of years when the rains failed and crops withered away.

We can now ship goods and food almost anywhere in the world in a matter of days following a catastrophe, giving us the opportunity to respond to disasters that affect our families, our neighbours, our countries and increasingly peoples in other parts of the world. The terrible tsunami of December 2004, the earthquake disaster in Pakistan in 2005, the massive floods in Mozambique of 2000 or the sight of starving people in Africa, capture our attention and elicit a response, however inadequate to the reality and horror of the situation. But, our efforts to help in the near future may be hampered by the sheer scale of the impact of climate change on our ability to grow food. We are now thousands of millions more people than we were even a century ago and, without radical action now to limit climate change, we could be seeing millions of refugees on an annual basis, with nowhere to go. We may have created cushions against catastrophe, but our vulnerability is as never before, just by the sheer dint of numbers involved and how close to the edge we are.

And what about a climate change prediction that we may or may not experience for decades? Do we act now to prevent a disaster that has barely touched the horizon, especially when some sceptics are telling us that the ups and downs in local weather are nothing more than the vagaries of a natural system, such as fluctuations in the energy received from the sun? Just how should we cater for a climate change event that hasn't yet happened or may not happen, if climatologists, with their models, have got it wrong? Some of us, because of some gut feeling that we can't continue consuming the resources of the planet in the way we do, may feel compelled to do something, like cutting back on holiday travel, using public transport or lowering the temperature of the central heating system, even though such gestures may be little more than token. The question is what we can do? What should we do?

If we believed that the climatologists were in the right ball park, that their projections were not wide of the mark, we would try sensibly to carry out a damage-limiting exercise through reducing greenhouse gas emissions, while not forgetting that the world's surviving ecosystems are vitally important as buffers against change. Or we could do nothing, as Bjørn Lomborg suggests in his book, *The Sceptical Environmentalist,* other than to help in the fight against global poverty through better trade agreements and through debt-forgiveness, all of which would be far more cost-effective, he claims, in helping humanity to survive the future than if we were to pitch out efforts in what would be nothing more than an inadequate attempt to hold back global warming.

But, even though Lomborg may have changed his tune, from a person in denial of human-induced climate change, he still fails to understand the full nature of what is happening. Like those who believe that changes in solar luminosity explain all, Lomborg does not understand that our persistence in consuming the Earth's natural resources, especially the remaining forests of the planet, is also a strong, vital component in the equation of climate change. The attempt to alleviate poverty, if not combined with an effort to reduce future climate trends, will prove a fearful waste of resources, while simultaneously failing to prevent a collapse of the Earth's essential life-support ecosystems.

What about the Earth's resources? Through advances in technology we have created modern consumer societies; through international trade and communication, managed by transnational companies, we have brought more and more of the world's population into the ambit of 'economic' development. The net result of all such activity is that we are reaching the limits of what the earth can provide or even exceeding them. A city such as London with its 7.5 million people requires the resources of a land mass more than one hundred times greater, that is, when we consider its needs for fresh water, energy and food. This 'ecological footprint' takes into account the watershed for providing water, the networks of roads and rail, energy in the form of electricity and fuels for transportation as well as the agricultural base, whether in the UK or abroad. If we were to take the needs of an average person living in London and multiply them by the world's population on the basis that what is good for a Londoner should be good for someone in India or China, then we would need the resources of several planets the size of the earth.

Obviously that cannot be: obviously something is wrong with an economic model of development based on the notion that the resources of our planet, combined with human technological ingenuity, can overcome any shortages in the fundamental necessities of life. Already, millions of people face shortages in fresh water, and the latest projections from bodies such as the World Wildlife Fund and the International Water Management Institute (IWMI), are for such shortages to become chronic as a result of climate change and global warming. Meanwhile, through the exigencies of the World Bank and the International Monetary Fund, more and more countries have been persuaded that self-sufficiency in food is unnecessary when cheaper food can be imported from elsewhere. But climate change and the ensuing water shortages may well put paid to food surpluses, and countries that have turned their backs on food self-sufficiency, could well find themselves in deep trouble when the food granaries of the world, such as the Corn Belt of the United States, dry up and fail as a result.

Meanwhile, agro-industry sees that much is to be gained from investing in crops for biofuels, whether to substitute for petrol and diesel, or to power electricity generators. The value of biofuels is mounting all the time as a 'green' and therefore 'good' fuel based on the notion that it is far more carbon neutral than petroleum or natural gas, and therefore likely to bring carbon emissions down, even in a world where demand for energy is increasing rapidly. But biofuels are far from being carbon neutral: they need fertile soils and large inputs of water, fertilizer and biocides, as well as transportation systems that can bring such crops to a central point for production and then distribution, all of which demands an investment in energy that currently is fossil fuel based.

Governments are also increasingly promoting the idea of energy crops without taking into account that a growing population needs food and freshwater. Where will that food be grown to sustain an increasingly urbanized population? Agro-industry gains both ways, first through the production of value added energy crops and second, because of such production, the generation of food scarcity.

The irony is that petroleum and natural gas have a few decades at best, given current and future demand, before consumption will exceed the discovery of new deposits. After that point in time, potential consumption of such fuels will exceed the energy industry's capacity to produce, and the costs of production will send prices rocketing up. From a purely economic point of view, biofuels would then come into their own.

The demand for energy is increasing everywhere in the world, despite improving efficiencies of use, such as motor vehicles that have double or triple the mileage per gallon compared with consumption a few years ago. Every time world energy consumption is doubled, in the region of a thirty year doubling time, more energy is consumed during the course of the next doubling than has ever been consumed over all time by humanity. How possibly can the world afford to fuel such growing demand?

Nuclear power is bandied around as one answer, on the erroneous basis that it is greenhouse emission neutral since its energy derives from splitting the atom. In the same breath, we are also being told that all we need to do is expand rapidly the power base of nuclear power stations, until maybe in forty years' time we will have 'fusion' reactors up and running. These 'options' are government-controlled, centralized options that will necessitate constant vigilance against acts of terrorism and acts of war between countries or even between factions in countries, where violent struggles for independence and domination are pursued. Just think how much the United States and European powers are suspicious of Iran's intentions in establishing a nuclear industry. Is Iran's nuclear programme for 'peaceful' purposes, and even were that so, could such a programme be easily converted into a military programme? Nor can safe operation be guaranteed, and just one major accident, on the scale of Chernobyl or worse, can make vast swathes of land unsafe for human beings over a century or more or even uninhabitable.

Nuclear power currently meets approximately 3 percent of the world's primary energy needs and consumes 60,000 tonnes of natural uranium, prior to any enrichment of the fuel. At that rate 'economically recoverable' reserves of uranium — about 10 million tonnes — would last less than one hundred years. A worldwide programme of 1000 nuclear reactors, hence three times the current proportion of nuclear power, would give us fifty years of uranium, and if the world's current demand for electricity were met by nuclear power, the uranium would last 4 years.

Although uranium is ubiquitous, the problem, once high grade ores have been used up, is the amount of energy, largely fossil fuel energy, which has to be invested in mining and extraction, given the rapid tailing off of good quality ores. Even with the good ores that are currently in use the energy gained compared to that invested over the lifetime of the reactor, including its decommissioning and safe nuclear waste disposal, is small at best. According to Jan Willem, Storm van Leeuwen and Philip Smith, in their analysis of energy inputs and outputs, the use of poorer grade uranium will result in net deficits in energy.

Far from being 'carbon neutral' as claimed by the nuclear industry nuclear power stations have been built and will be built on the back of the fossil fuel industry. The extraction of uranium from mines, its processing, its transportation, quite likely from Australia or Canada, its enrichment in fissionable uranium, its manufacture into metal-clad fuel rods, and then the construction of the nuclear reactor, with its massive concrete containment, are all fossil-fuel supported activities, as indeed is the management of spent nuclear fuel and finally the decommissioning of the reactor.

In the light of climate change and global warming, the UK government is currently in the midst of a propaganda campaign to persuade the public that its has no option but to accept nuclear power. In June 2005, Malcolm Wicks, UK energy minister, told the Welsh Affairs Select Committee that 'the British nuclear industry will build new nuclear power stations without direct state subsidies so long as the government sets a high price on carbon-polluting electricity.' And he added that, 'the government will commit itself to a framework that sets a long-term price for carbon, either through a domestic, EU-wide or eventually wider international trading agreement.'

Such statements are intentionally misleading. If all the carbon emissions associated with the production of nuclear power generated electricity were taken into account, the taxes on those emissions would push up the cost of nuclear power accordingly. Nuclear power generation costs are not independent of fossil fuel costs and they are unlikely to be so.

Decisions we take today, whether to opt for nuclear power, will determine the future. The immense investment required to fuel the world's energy needs from the atom means essentially putting alternative ways of raising and using energy on the back burner. As has been pointed out innumerable times, investment in energy efficiency, all the way down the line from how the electricity is generated to the moment when the consumer flicks on the switch, is many times more cost-effective than building costly nuclear power stations, or indeed large power stations of any type.

Clearly efficiency on its own can never be the whole answer: we will always need to generate electricity. But, today, we have an enormous advantage compared with fifty years ago. We now have electronic technology that can switch smoothly and effectively between 'end-use' needs and actual electricity generation. Such switching systems are ideally suited for combining different mini-sources of power at low cost in real terms. Critics of renewable energy systems such as wind-power, photovoltaics or wave-power, quite rightly point out that such systems are 'intermittent' and relatively speaking 'unpredictable' compared with a coal-fired or even nuclear power generating facility.

What if we were to get away from the concept and operation of an all-dominating central grid system with large power stations transmitting electricity all over the country? Isolated, central grid power stations, including nuclear reactors, lose as much as two-thirds of the energy generated in the cooling systems. Instead of such grossly inefficient systems, we could build up localized, embedded electricity generation that switches between intermittent sources, such as wind generating systems, and combined heat and power plants (CHP). CHP plants can be designed to burn natural gas (methane) or locally derived biofuels to give both electricity and heat for local industries and households. Meanwhile, any excess electricity in the system, for instance when the wind blows, can be put into storage systems such as a heating circuit with its storage tank or into batteries of electric cars. That would maximize the gains from the system.

In end-use terms, such embedded localized systems are twice or more as efficient as electricity generated from far afield. They are also independent of imports, whether of coal, natural gas or uranium, therefore giving security of supply, and they offer no targets worth the making to terrorists or other would-be aggressors. Not least, such embedded systems do not put the country at risk from reactor accidents.

Ideally, we would use an electronic switching device to provide a smooth transition, when necessary, from one generating source to the other, using the combined heat and power plant as an important, work-horse back up. In the home and factory, another switching device, such as developed for mini-hydro electricity generating systems, would enable the user to limit the electricity required at any one moment. The switching device would shuffle electricity around such that the refrigerator, for example, would be switched off, when someone is ironing or hoovering. The electricity supplier would benefit enormously from such a system, as it would smooth out the peaks in demand and reduce the need for power plants waiting in the wings for sudden surges. The consumer would benefit from substantially lowered costs in real terms.

And, were there to be a time when electric vehicles had become the norm, the switching device could shuffle power to heat systems, such as heat storage cookers and boilers, as well as the charging of batteries when other needs had dwindled, as during the night. If we were able to have such a system at our disposal, then in one stroke we would be saving as much as half on the average amount of primary energy used today. Such embedded, combined, electronically controlled systems would be virtually carbon neutral.

Meanwhile, we waste enormous quantities of electricity in maintaining our appliances, such as television sets, hi-fi systems, washing machines and computers, in state of stand-by. As a result, states DEFRA, the Department for the Environment, Food and Rural Affairs, the UK emits an extra one million tonnes of carbon emissions. That is enough electricity to power the needs of 400,000

homes, and if all such devices were turned off when not in use, we could reduce electricity requirements by the equivalent of one large-sized generation plant.

Across the world, every locality would have its own 'take' on the system, whether photovoltaics in sunny climes, wind machines in windy locations, wave and tide machines where such devices make sense, and all could have a biofuel-back up system, including one that generated methane for cooking and other direct-use purposes.

Agriculture, too, needs again to become 'embedded' such as to provide the needs of localized populations, not only in terms of food products, but also in providing energy, as in biofuels. Farmers' markets should not be on the fringes of society, but central to its needs.

Without question we will need all the ingenuity at our disposal to prevent climatic disaster, while somehow alleviating poverty and misery for a growing world population. We must learn again to become resourceful and as far as is possible, self-reliant, although

we now have the distinct advantage, through trade and communication, that we can respond quickly to the needs of communities in distress because of some environmental disaster, including the impact of climate change.

What is becoming increasingly certain is that we cannot hope to survive if we continue rampaging across the planet, as if we owned it. James Lovelock is right to talk about the revenge of Gaia. We are utterly dependent on the earth's ecosystems to maintain equilibrium, to help distribute energy across the length and breadth of the surface of the earth. Greenhouse gas emissions and the resulting global warming are part of the problem, particularly in pushing up against tipping points, but our preoccupation with global warming must be tempered by a proper understanding of the role of global ecosystems, such as polar regions and the tropics, and not least the Amazon rainforests.

We still have time, but only if we act effectively now.

*Sunset, Swifts Creek, Victoria, Australia, May 2006  [Peter Firus]*

# Reading List and Sources

Barrett, P. (2005/06) Editorial, *Pacific Ecologist,* 11, pp.6–8.

Betts R.A., P.M. Cox, S.E. Lee and F.I. Woodward (1997) 'Contrasting physiological structural vegetation feedbacks in climate change simulations,' *Nature,* 387, pp.796–99.

Betts, R.A. (2001) 'Forests, Soils and Global Warming,' *RSA,* Lecture Notes, February 21.

Betts, R.A., Cox, P.M., Collins, M., Gash, J.H.C., Harris, P.P., Huntingford, C., Jones, C.D., and Williams, K.D. (2002) *Amazonian forest die-back in the Hadley Centre coupled climate-vegetation model.* UK Meteorological Office, Hadley Centre.

Branford, Sue (2005) 'Running on Empty,' *The Guardian,* November 2.

Boyle, Godfrey, Everett, B. and Ramage, J. (2003) eds., *Energy Systems and Sustainability,* OUP.

Boyle, Godfrey (2004) ed. *Renewable Energy,* OUP, UK.

Bunyard, Peter (1996) ed. *Gaia in Action: Science of the Living Earth,* Floris Books, Edinburgh.

—, (1999) *The Breakdown of Climate: Human Choices or Global Disaster,* Floris Books, Edinburgh.

—, (2001) 'The Climate Crisis,' *The Ecologist,* Vol. 31, 9.

—, (2005) 'Destroying the Amazon,' *More 4 News Opinion,* December 2.

—, (2005/2) 'Climate and the Amazon,' *More 4 News.* December 9.

—, (2006) 'This trade in carbon emissions won't combat global warming,' *The Guardian,* July 21.

Caffrey, Andy (2006) 'Antarctica's Deep Impact Threat,' *Climate Action NOW!* January 18.

Cochrane, M.A., Alencar, A., Schulze, M.D., Souza, C.M.,Jr., Nepstad, D.C., Lefebvre, P., and Davidson, E.A. (1999) 'Positive Feedbacks in the Fire Dynamic of Closed Canopy Tropical Forests,' *Science,* 284, 11 June, pp.1832–1835.

Cochrane, M.A. and Laurance, W.F. (2002) 'Fire as a large-scale edge effect in Amazonian forests,' *Journal of Tropical Ecology,* 18, pp.311–325.

Cowling, S.A., Maslin, M.A., and Sykes, M.T. (2001) 'Paleovegetation Simulations of Lowland Amazonia and Implications for Neotropical Allopatry and Speciation,' *Quaternary Research,* 55, pp.140–49.

Cox, P.M., Betts, R.A., Jones, C., Spall, S.A., Totterdel, I.A. (2000) 'Acceleration of global-warming due to carbon-cycle feedbacks in a coupled climate model,' *Nature, Letters,* 408, Nov 9.

Diamond, Jared (2006) *Collapse: How Societies Choose to Fail or Survive,* Allen Lane, Penguin UK.

Environment News Service (2006) 'Amazon Drought Worst in 100 Years,' January 19.

Fearnside, P.M. (1997) 'Greenhouse Gases from Deforestation in Brazilian Amazonia: Net Committed Emissions,' *Climatic Change,* 35, (3) pp.321–60.

—, (2000) 'Global warming and tropical land-use change: greenhouse gas emissions from biomass burning, decomposition and soils in forest conversion, shifting cultivation and secondary vegetation,' *Climatic Change,* 46, pp.115–58.

Gawith, M.J., T.E. Downing, and T.S. Karacostas (1999) 'Heatwaves in a changing climate,' in *Climate, Change and Risk,* Downing, T.E., A.J. Olsthoorn, and R.S.J. Tol (eds.), Routledge, London, UK, pp.279–307.

Gedney, N. and Valdes, P.J. (2000) 'The Effect of Amazonian deforestation on the northern hemisphere circulation and climate,' *Geophysical Research Letters,* 27, pp.3053–56.

Goldsmith, Edward (1998) *The Way: an Ecological World-View,* Georgia University Press.

Grace, J. (1996) 'Forests and the Global Carbon Cycle,' *S.It.E. Atti, 17*, pp.7–11.

Harding, Stephan (2006) *Animate Earth: Science, Intuition and Gaia,* Green Books, UK.

Henriquez, M. (2006) IDEAM, Colombia, *personal communication,* August.

Holdren, J. (2006) 'Top Scientist's fears for climate,' *BBC News,* August 31.

Institute of Science in Society (2006) *Which Energy?* 2006 Energy Report, *ISIS,* March.

Laurance, W.F. and Williamson, G.B. (2001) 'Positive feedbacks among forest fragmentation, drought, and climate change in the Amazon,' *Conserv. Biol., 15,* pp.1529–35.

Lean, J. and Rowntree, P.R. (1993) 'A GCM simulation of Amazonian deforestation on climate using an improved canopy representation,' *Q.J.R. Meteol. Soc.,* 119, pp.509–30.

Levin, Kelly and Pershing, Jonathan (2006) *Climate Science 2005. Major New Discoveries,* World Resources Institute, US.

Lomborg, Bjørn (2001) *The Sceptical Environmentalist,* CUP 2001.

Lovelock, James (1991) *Healing Gaia. Practical Medicine for the Planet,* Harmony Books, UK.

—, (2006) *The Revenge of Gaia,* Allen Lane, Penguin UK.

Lynas, Mark (2004) *High Tide. The Truth about our Climate Crisis,* Picador, USA.

—, (2005) *High Tide. News from a Warming World,* HarperCollins.

Maslin, Mark (2002) *The Coming Storm,* Barron's, Quarto US.

—, (2004) *Global Warming. A very short introduction*, OUP, UK.

Molion, L.C. (1989) 'The Amazonian Forests and Climatic Stability,' *The Ecologist,* 19, No.6.

Pielke, R.A. (2002) *Mesoscale meteorological modeling,* 2nd Edition, Academic Press, San Diego, CA.

Poveda, G., Waylen, P.R., Pulwarty, R.S. (2006) 'Annual and inter-annual variability of the present climate in northern South America and southern Meso-America,' *Palaeo,* article in press.

Ray, D. K., Nair U.S., Lawton R.O., Welch R.M., Pielke R.A. Sr. (2006) 'Impact of land use on Costa Rican tropical montane cloud forests: Sensitivity of orographic cloud formation to deforestation in the plains,' *Journal of Geophysical Research,* Vol.111.

Salati, E. (1987) 'The Forest and the Hydrological Cycle,' in *The Geophysiology of Amazonia,* Dickinson, R.E., ed., Wiley Interscience.

UK Meteorological Office (2005) *Avoiding Dangerous Climate Change,* February 1–3.

Werth, D. and Avissar, R. (2002) 'The local and global effects of Amazon deforestation,' *Journal of Geophysical Research,* 107.

Willem, Jan, Storm van Leeuwen and Philip Smith (2005) *Nuclear Power: the Energy Balance,* University of Groningen.

# Index